The Trans-Chaco Highway

How It Came to Be

Gerhard Ratzlaff

Translated by Richard Ratzlaff,
Toronto, Canada

Asunción, Paraguay, 2009

THE BEGINNING OF THE WESTERN PART OF THE TRANS-CHACO HIGHWAY

Villa Hayes to Filadelfia

Distance: 398 kilometers

Built with cooperation among

The Government of Paraguay   The Government of the United States of America

Mennonite Central Committee - The Cattle Ranchers of the Chaco

Cover Photograph: The Trans-Chaco Highway today, 2009

© Gerhard Ratzlaff 2009 Asunción, Paraguay
First published in German 1998
English translation by Richard Ratzlaff, Toronto, Canada

Printed in Paraguay

ISBN: 978-99953-2-192-5

Dedicated to:

William T. Snyder and Harry Harder

- for Biblically grounded development assistance,
- for bread not shaped like loaves

Contents

The Trans-Chaco Highway: A Timeline 9

Abbreviations 11

Foreword by Edgar Stoesz 13

Introduction 15

1. The Paraguayan Chaco and Law 514 19
2. The Mennonites Make Their Way into the Chaco Wilderness 23
3. Early Methods of Transportation among the Mennonites in the Chaco 30
4. A Travel Report from Early Days 34
5. MCC in Search of a Secure Future for Fellow Believers in Paraguay 43
6. A Memorandum 47
7. The Critical Situation of the Mennonites in the Chaco: "To Be or Not to Be" 49
8. The Inspiring Example of Harry Harder 53
9. Vern Buller – A "Modern Prophet" 58
10. It All Began with a Stomach Operation 62
11. Vern Buller Looks Back 66
12. President Stroessner Visits the Chaco Mennonite Colonies (November 12, 1954) 73
13. A Study of the Chaco 77
14. The Efforts of MCC for a Trans-Chaco Highway 82
15. Gustav Storm 96
16. Decree No. 13.965, August 3, 1955 99
17. Robert Eaton and the Chaco Cattle Ranchers 102

18.	US Involvement: Point IV in Paraguay	108
19.	A Demonstration and Training Project	112
20.	The Agreement between the US Government and MCC	116
21.	Harry Harder Builds the Trans-Chaco Highway	119
22.	"The Trans-Chaco Highway Is Ready"	134
23.	"The Servant Has Done His Duty …"	136
24.	A Devastating Judgment: Project Performance Unsatisfactory	142
25.	The Experiences of the PAX Men on the Trans-Chaco Highway	147
26.	The Trans-Chaco Highway in the Context of a Practical Theology	163
27.	Conclusion and Evaluation	172
28.	A Personal Note in Conclusion	176
	Bibliography	182

The Trans-Chaco Highway: A Timeline

1921, May	A Mennonite Expedition from Canada explores the Chaco.
1921, July 26	Law 514 setting out the settlement of Mennonites in the Chaco is passed.
1927	Menno Colony is established: the first settlement of Mennonites in the Chaco.
1930	Fernheim Colony is established by refugees from Russia.
1947	Neuland Colony is established by refugees from Russia.
1951, Aug. 24	A memorandum from J. W. Fretz to the director of Point IV. The first concrete proposal for a Trans-Chaco Highway project.
1952	Harry Harder brings a bulldozer to Paraguay from the US. He first builds a road for Volendam and Friesland in East Paraguay and when that work is complete (1953), brings the bulldozer to the Chaco.
1953, June 11	Vern Buller offers to come with 40 tons of road-building equipment to build roads in the Chaco.
1954	TAM (the Paraguayan Military Air Transport service) begins weekly flights to the Chaco colonies.
1954–1955	In less than a year Vern Buller builds about 135 kilometers of road in the Chaco.
1954–1955	MCC invests a great deal of energy promoting the building of the Trans-Chaco Highway.
1954, Nov. 12	President Alfredo Stroessner visits Filadelfia with a large entourage and promises undertaking the building of the Trans-Chaco highway.
1954, Nov. 22	A large national and international delegation visits the Chaco to observe the progress made by Vern Buller building roads.

1955, Feb. 28	A Commission for a highway from Filadelfia to Villa Hayes is established.
1955, May 18	A Road Construction Project Agreement is signed between USOM/Paraguay and MOPC.
1955, June 18	A Demonstration and Training Project Agreement is signed between USOM/P and MOPC.
1955, July 13	The Commission for the building of the Trans-Chaco highway is appointed, with representatives from MOPC, FOA, the cattle ranchers of the Chaco, and the Mennonites.
1955, Aug. 3	Decree 13.965 authorizes the establishment of the Trans-Chaco Road Building Commission for the purpose of building the highway.
1956, June 3	An agreement is signed between Paraguay and the U.S. to build the Trans-Chaco highway.
1956, Sept. 1	An agreement is signed between ICA and MCC. ICA will survey the route, MCC will build the road.
1956, Nov.	Construction of the Ruta Trans-Chaco begins with the stretch from Jardin Botanico to Piguete Cue (24 km).
1957, Feb.	Construction of the Ruta Trans-Chaco itself begins at Villa Hayes.
1957	MCC arranges for a credit of US $1 million for the Mennonites in the Chaco and Friesland and Volendam colonies in East Paraguay.
1961, Oct. 4	The Trans-Chaco Highway is completed to the Mennonite colonies.
1964, Sept. 10	The Trans-Chaco Highway is completed to the Bolivian border.
1991	The paving of the Trans-Chaco Highway is completed from Asunción to Filadelfia.

Abbreviations

AID	Agency for International Development (US)
CSEM	Mennonite Social and Economic Committee (Paraguay)
FOA/P	Foreign Operations Administration/Paraguay (US)
ICA	International Cooperation Administration (forerunner of AID)
MCC	Mennonite Central Committee (Akron, Pennsylvania)
MEDA	Mennonite Economic Development Associates
MOPC	Ministry of Public Works and Communication (Paraguay)
STICA	Inter-American Technical Service for Agricultural Cooperation
TAM	The Military Air Transport (Transporte Aereo Militar, Paraguay)
USAID	United States AID Mission to Paraguay
USOM/P	United States Operation Mission to Paraguay

Foreword

"The Trans-Chaco Highway: How It Came To Be" tells a large and fascinating story. Mennonites had staked everything on settling the Paraguayan Chaco. They went there with courage, firmly convinced that it was God's will. The first few years were indescribably difficult however. After 25 years, when they still had made virtually no economic progress, many became discouraged and emigrated to Canada or Germany. Even the most optimistic came to wonder if there was a future for them in the Chaco.

More and more settlers came to the conclusion that there had to be an end to the isolation of the Chaco, if there was to be any hope of economic progress. But how? Extending the railway from Km 145 into the colonies was not a solution to the problem of finding markets for the colonies' products. Even regular air service, which began in 1954 and made it easier for persons to travel, was only a partial solution. A Trans-Chaco Highway, running through the wild uninhabited Chaco from the colonies directly to Asunción, however, appeared in the 1950s to be a dream, a utopian hope.

But the dream became reality in a stunningly short space of time. This book tells the captivating story of how this miracle came about. With painstaking research, Ratzlaff has unearthed the beginnings of what finally came to be the project for a Trans-Chaco Highway. It was an "unlikely coalition" between the Paraguayan and US governments, the Mennonite Central Committee, and the Mennonites and cattle ranchers of the Chaco that brought this unique, exceptional project to completion.

The highway from Asunción to the Mennonite colonies was completed within five years. Today, now that the highway is paved, transport trucks, busses, and private cars drive at speeds rivaling those on German Autobahns. It is easy to forget the enormous efforts that were necessary [10] to build this highway. It is the achievement of this book to remind us of this almost forgotten but vital chapter in the history of Mennonites in Paraguay.

Ratzlaff does not want only to tell the story of how the Trans-Chaco highway came to be. It is his sincere wish to show that the building of the highway was an example of biblically grounded development assistance in practice. Indeed, it is possible to do Christian service even on a bulldozer.

The Trans-Chaco highway was a decisive factor in the economic development of the Mennonite colonies in the Chaco. Today the Mennonites are making great efforts to pass on to their neighbors the gift of aid that they received from their brothers and sisters in faith, in the form of projects of Christian service and missions. This is commendable.

The list of names of those who took part in the construction of the Trans-Chaco highway is long. But two persons especially need to be acknowledged by name: Harry Harder and William T. Snyder. Harder understood how to work with large machinery and unskilled young people; in an extreme climate and under very challenging environmental conditions, he brought the construction of the highway to a successful conclusion. Snyder was in a position to put together that "unlikely coalition" and to keep it together through some severe crises. May his memory be honored!

The saga of the Trans-Chaco Highway: How It Came to Be is worth telling, and this book has told the story.

Edgar Stoesz

long-time MCC Director for Latin America
Akron, Pennsylvania, February, 1998

Introduction

The Trans-Chaco highway, which begins in Asunción and crosses the Paraguayan Chaco through the Mennonite settlements and extends to the Bolivian border, is the lifeline of the Paraguayan Chaco, especially of the central Chaco and the Mennonite colonies, Menno, Fernheim, and Neuland. Over the past several decades these have developed into the most productive centers of the entire South American Chaco.[1]

An indication of the economic significance of the Trans-Chaco Highway for the Mennonite colonies can be found in data [1997] such as the following: The three Mennonite colonies, with 13,000 inhabitants, own approximately 1.3 million hectares of land in the Chaco, which is 5.2% of the Paraguayan Chaco and 3.2% of all of Paraguay. These three colonies in the Chaco produce 50% of the country's milk products, 11% of the meat (approximately 120,000 head of cattle per year), and nearly 30% of peanuts and 5% of the cotton grown in the country.

On October 22–23, 1997, Fernheim meat producers participated in a countrywide fair for beef cattle in Asunción. Mennonite cattle ranchers from the Chaco took first and second place. There are more than 4,000 motorized vehicles (cars and pickups) and approximately 150 freight trucks with a capacity of 25 tons each (the limit for the Trans-Chaco highway), which make about 10,000 trips each year with goods from the colonies to Asunción. Approximately 180,000 tons of products are shipped each year on the highway.[2]

The national per capita income per year for Paraguay is US $1,600. In the Mennonite colonies it is US $10,000.

The Mennonite colonies are the trade and business center of the Chaco for cattle ranchers and the military. They are the shopping center for travelers and lately have become more and more a tourist attraction.

---

[1] *See the "Suplemento Especial" [special supplement], ABC-Color (November 25, 1997), p. 4.*
[2] *Figures provided by Heinrich Dyck, Executive Secretary of the council of mayors of the Mennonite colonies in Paraguay, Comité Social y Económico Mennonita (C.S.E.M.); additional information from "Schlachtochsenwettbewerb" [Prize Beef Contest], Mennoblatt (November 16, 1997), p. 16.*

The above data reveal clearly the economic prosperity of the Mennonites in the Chaco. How were they able to achieve such amazing success in this remote Chaco wilderness? This question is asked repeatedly by national and international visitors.

A number factors contributed to this success, including diligence, perseverance, solidarity, cooperation, and reasonable lines of credit from foreign sources in the 1950s and 60s. An extremely important factor remains, however, the construction of the Trans-Chaco highway. Without it the economic progress achieved would have been unthinkable. The significance of this road for the development of the entire Chaco is evident everywhere. [13] The intent of this book is to illustrate how the Trans-Chaco highway project came about and how the road was built. I focus here especially on the contribution of the Mennonites to this project as well as – and this was one of my primary motives for this research project – the historical and religious forces that motivated and animated this monumental effort.

Robert Eaton (see chapter 16), the American cattle rancher in the Chaco who had a great interest in the construction of the Trans-Chaco Highway and participated actively in the planning stages of the project, told me in a personal conversation, "The initiative for the construction of the road came from the Mennonites. Without their efforts it would not have been built." In this book it is not my primary purpose to determine whether Mr. Eaton's statement is true. I simply want to describe the participation of the Mennonites in the development and construction of the Trans-Chaco Highway. I deliberately focus especially on the work and the efforts of the Mennonite Central Committee (MCC) and the Mennonites in the Chaco.

By far the largest part of this book deals with the origin and development of the Trans-Chaco highway project. Because of the lack of documentation, less attention is given to the practical and technical aspects of the project. In chapter 26 I point briefly to what motivated this project: historical and theological forces that were never made explicit and seem almost invisible behind this huge and expensive project – a 450-year history of mutual aid which is emphasized and carried out from within a living Biblical faith [14] in spite of many mistakes and failures on the part of those participating. It is certainly Biblical when the truth about construction of the Trans-Chaco highway is brought out from "under the bushel." Even more so because today very few know about the contribution of MCC and the Mennonites in planning and carrying out the construction of the highway. It is my intention to fill this gap. In addition, the tradition of mutual aid which was the motivating factor in this project is highlighted in order to motivate the present-day readers to practice charity in the same Christian spirit. It is worth serving "In the Name of Christ."

It was not easy to gather materials for this work. There are many gaps in the story and it lacks a consistent style and structure. It could be compared to a mosaic, in which many small, colorful pieces are put together to form a picture. The intended audience for the original German edition of this work was the Mennonites in Paraguay. [I trust that this English translation will interest Mennonites from around the world who come to Paraguay for the Mennonite World Conference in 2009.]

I owe special thanks to the following people: Frank J. Wiens was MCC Director in Paraguay for many years and encouraged MCC to send me the correspondence that is the basis of the book. Edgar Stoesz, MCC Director for Latin America for many years, went to great effort in his Zusammenarbeit ("cooperation"), an expression he used often in our relationship. He sent me additional material and arranged for former Pax men to send me reminiscences of their time working on the Trans-Chaco highway (I am happy to say that each one who responded encouraged me to write this book). Gundolf Niebuhr, archivist of Fernheim Colony, sent me a list of all the articles on the Trans-Chaco highway published in the Mennoblatt. [15] Michael Rudolph and Camilla Tabbert, German teachers in the Mennonite schools in Paraguay, checked the original German text for grammatical accuracy. During their corrections they took care to preserve the peculiarities of my Paraguayan Mennonite German. This was not always easy for them. The cooperation of my wife, Luise, was very valuable to me. She stood by my side throughout the entire work. She did most of the typing, carefully read the text, and gave me valuable suggestions that helped me avoid a number of mistakes. This work is therefore the fruit of practical, "sisterly/brotherly" (geschwisterlichen Zusammenarbeit) cooperation.

Gerhard Ratzlaff
Asunción, Paraguay
1998

1
The Paraguayan Chaco and Law 514

Without the privileges guaranteed in Bill 514 the Mennonites would not have come to the Chaco; conversely, Bill 514 most likely would not have passed if the Mennonites had asked to settle anywhere else but in the Paraguayan Chaco. In the debates on the privileges asked for by the Mennonites there were two main issues that weighed in favor of the privileges being granted: the Chaco had not yet been opened for settlement and the boundary with Bolivia was not yet established.

On July 12, 1921, Bill 514 regarding the privileges for the Mennonites who wanted to settle in Paraguay was debated in the Paraguayan Senate. A number of senators spoke against the statute. They felt that the privileges, especially the exemption from military service for the immigrating Mennonites and their descendants, were in direct conflict with the Paraguayan constitution. Others were skeptical about the Mennonite Waisenamt, the Office for Orphans, since the rules governing inheritance in the colonies would be administered by this office. Another group of senators was opposed to granting Mennonites the right to have their own schools with instruction in German. They argued that this would prevent the group from integrating into Paraguayan society. The greatest concern was that the Mennonites could develop into a state within a state with its own laws and government, contrary to the interests of the Paraguayan state.

The defenders of the Mennonite bill had weighty arguments in their favor, which had to do with the unique character of the Chaco:

- The Chaco is an unsettled desert, a place where Paraguayans do not wish to go, much less to settle there. This was strongly emphasized by Senator F. C. Chaves.
- The Mennonites had a history of successful colonization, beginning in Holland, then from Prussia to Russia and Canada. This was evidence enough that they could be counted on to colonize and develop the infamous Chaco and that in the course of time they would become good Paraguayans of Mennonite faith.

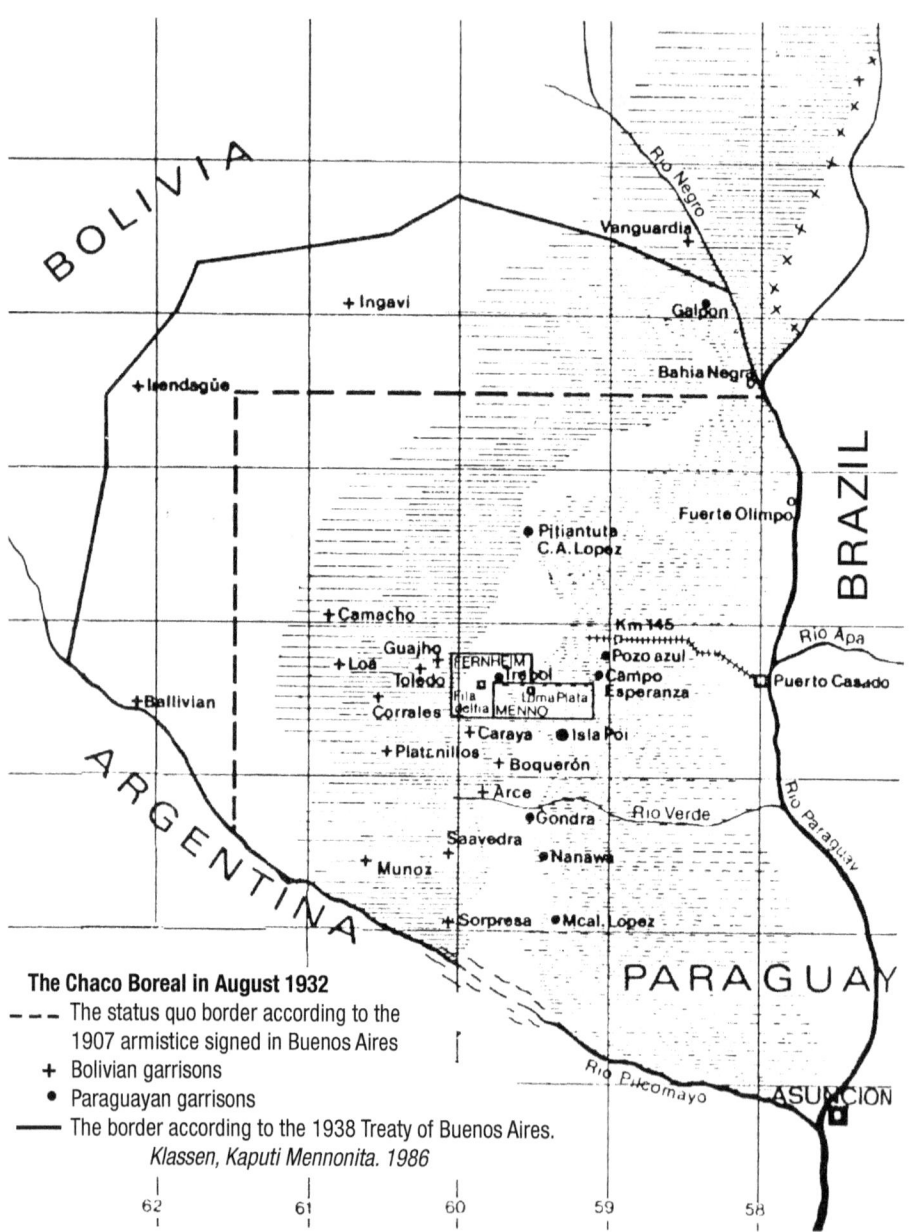

The Chaco Boreal in August 1932
- - - The status quo border according to the 1907 armistice signed in Buenos Aires
+ Bolivian garrisons
• Paraguayan garrisons
——— The border according to the 1938 Treaty of Buenos Aires.
Klassen, Kaputi Mennonita. 1986

- The Minister of the Interior, representing the government before the Senate, emphasized strongly that the development of the Chaco by the Mennonites would strengthen the Paraguayan claim to sovereignty over the Chaco in opposition to Bolivia, which also claimed sovereignty over the area. "Esta es la cuestión." "This is the issue."

The Mennonites did not know this at the time, but the undefined border between Paraguay and Bolivia worked to their advantage and the bill was passed.[3]

The press reacted sharply against the special privileges for the Mennonites. Paraguay's largest daily newspaper, *La Tribuna*, was especially aggressive in its criticism, running headlines against the Mennonite statute like the following: "Un proyecto monstruoso," (A monstrous project) "Pueblo, la patria está en peligro," (People, your fatherland is in danger), "La venta del País ha sido efectuada" (This is how our country has been sold). *El Liberal*, on the other hand, defended the special privileges for the Mennonites. It pointed out that this was in the country's interests and praised extravagantly the good reputation of the Mennonites: "We need immigrants, we need farmers and the Mennonites are the best kind of people. They are peace-loving, hard-working people who will respect the laws of the country" (June 10, 1921). *El Liberal* stated with prophetic earnestness:

A field of bitter grass and a bottle tree. (Quiring, 1936)

---

[3] *See on this matter the two booklets of Gerhard Ratzlaff, Entre dos Fuegos (1993), and Immigración y Colonización de los Mennonitas en el Paraguay bajo Ley 514 (1993).*

"They will build a city in the Chaco, not a state within a state, and we will go there to visit them. All those who hunger and thirst for righteousness will go there to see this Mennonite city, where the motto of our flag, 'Peace and Justice,' burns in the hearts of its citizens, who honor the name of God and do not want to shed the blood of their neighbor, nor their enemy, and who do not enrich themselves at the expense of their neighbor." (July 22, 1921)

Had the region to be settled not been the infamous Chaco, it is most unlikely that special privileges for the Mennonites would not have been granted. As the debate on Bill 514 shows, people were aware of how problematic it was to grant special privileges to a specific group of people. But the determining factor in the positive decision in favor of the Mennonites was surely the argument that settling Mennonites in the Chaco would secure the Chaco against Bolivia's claim. A further compelling argument was that in the long run even a self-contained colony would promote the economic integration of the Chaco.

"The field of the cross." This marks the farthest point reached, on May 20, by the Mennonite expedition of 1921, 320 km from Puerto Casado. As a memorial, they nailed a cross to a tree. (Quiring, 1936)

2

The Mennonites Make Their Way into the Chaco Wilderness

When the Mennonites came to this wilderness, the Chaco was an area avoided by European settlers. In fact, all previous attempts to settle the Chaco had been unsuccessful. What is today Villa Hayes used to be "a place of exile called Villa Occidental."[4] There were only a few small settlements along the Paraguay River. Under these circumstances and since there were no roads leading to their settlement area it seemed like an irresponsible and arrogant undertaking on the part of the Mennonites to settle in the middle of the Chaco. Did the special privileges given them by the government guarantee success? Would they be in a position to build the roads that many had dreamed of?

On December 31, 1926 the first 309 Mennonite settlers arrived in Puerto Casado. They had hoped to continue their journey to their land by train as they had been promised in 1921. But they were bitterly disappointed. To their great surprise they discovered that the railway had only been extended by 17 kilometers since 1921. This stretch of railway did not lead them closer to their settlement area but branched off to the south, towards Pirizal, altogether 77 kilometers from Puerto Casado; there was still a distance of more than 100 kilometers through the roadless wilderness to the land where they would settle.

The immediate concern of the settlers was how to keep going. The situation became even more desperate when they discovered that the land they had purchased had not yet been surveyed. Contrary to their intentions, some of them had to wait more than a year in Puerto Casado, which had devastating consequences. The unfamiliar and inadequate living conditions in the burning tropical sun brought sickness and even death to many. When the immigrants were finally able to settle their land in 1928, 194 people, 11% of their number, had died. Their situation seemed so hopeless

---

[4] See Hack, *Die Kolonisation der Mennoniten im paraguayischen Chaco (Amsterdam, 1961), pp. 21–26: "Der paraguayische Chaco als Siedlungsgebiet"* (the Paraguayan Chaco as a destination for settlers).

that of the original 270 families, 60 that had the means to do so (18.5%) left Puerto Casado and returned to Canada. Because of this, emigration from Canada to Paraguay slowed sharply. Would the great settlement undertaking in the Chaco be doomed to failure from the beginning? For most of the settlers, however, there was no turning back; they were condemned to stay. They had to go forward, by hook or crook, with ox carts over the grassy plain, through the thorny bush, through trackless wastes and with little hope of any secure existence in the near future.

On February 17, 1927, a few bold souls – six families and twelve young men – set out from Puerto Casado into the middle of the "Green Hell." They traveled the 77 kilometers to Pirizal on the narrow-gauge railway. There they transferred to the tall two-wheeled Paraguayan ox carts that were driven by native Paraguayans. At a snail's pace of barely 15 kilometers a day they wound their way, arriving in Pozo Azul (Blue Well) after a week that seemed endless. They had traveled 100 kilometers west from Pirizal. Here they set up a temporary settlement camp. Other families steadily followed. At the end of 1927 there were about 100 families that, like nomads in the trackless, strange and hostile Chaco wilderness, had settled temporarily in the wilderness.[5]

The first group on their way to the Chaco (Quiring, 1938)

---

[5] *For more information, see* Im Dienste der Gemeinschaft *[In the service of the community], published by the leadership of Menno Colony on the occasion of the 68th anniversary of the founding of Menno in the Chaco, June 25, 1995.*

2. The Mennonites Make Their Way into the Chaco Wilderness

Pioneers in the wilderness (Quiring, 1938)

The move into the Chaco was made group by group, each group consisting of five to six families. It was a time-consuming undertaking because many families had brought plows and other agricultural tools along with their household goods. In Pirizal the 100 wagons that had been brought from Canada were unpacked and reassembled and made ready for transporting the goods. Many families had no wagon and in other cases one wagon was not enough to move a family with all its possessions. Many families needed three wagons, which meant three trips. A motorized all-terrain vehicle with trailer, provided by the American settlement company (Intercontinental Company), was a big help. This company was the intermediary that had sold the land to the Mennonites at an inflated price.[6] They felt some responsibility for the success of this settlement and so made this all-terrain vehicle available to the settlers at no cost. This was a great help but was no substitute for the ox cart when it came to moving all of the goods.

Each stage of the trip had to be carefully planned. Above all, enough food had to be taken along, which was not easy. This consisted of dried noodles and toasted bread, hard tack, rice and beans, which were often wormy. Because the environment was strange to the newcomers the trips were organized so that each new group was led by someone who had already made the trip at least once. Over time a few brave young men distinguished themselves by willingly making many of these trips. Families

---

[6] It was purchased for US $3.13 and sold to the Mennonites for US $12.50. For more, see Walter Quiring, *Rußlanddeutsche suchen eine Heimat: Die deutsche Einwanderung in den paraguayischen Chaco* [Russian Germans in search of a home: The German migration into the Paraguayan Chaco] (Karlsruhe, 1938), chapter 8: "Ein verlustreiches Landgeschäft" [A money-losing land deal], pp. 61–66.

In the middle of the bush (Quiring, 1938)

with many children were concerned about what lay ahead and needed the support of these young men more than others. "Sometimes one saw a young mother, with frightened children gathered around her, sitting in the wagon, weeping quietly, when the wagon got stuck in the mud, not moving no matter how hard the oxen pulled." [7]

This source continues (in my lightly edited version): "The young men, who had often traveled the wilderness path they themselves had made and knew what lay ahead of them, saw the situation with much less concern. They encouraged the mothers and children and did everything they could to make the hardships of the trips easier to endure. When the time came for a period of rest the young men immediately went to work. They made a fire, prepared a hearty meal and did everything they could to cheer up the discouraged travelers. They also showed the people how to prepare themselves for a night's rest and how to protect themselves from mosquitoes and insects. They were already familiar with the valuable properties of the palo santo wood which could be found everywhere, burnt well, even when wet, and was therefore very valuable to the travelers." [8]

In the midst of many discouragements there also were some lighter moments, which let them forget their care and distress for a short while.

---

[7] *Im Dienste der Gemeinschaft*, June 25 995, p. 8.
[8] Ibid.

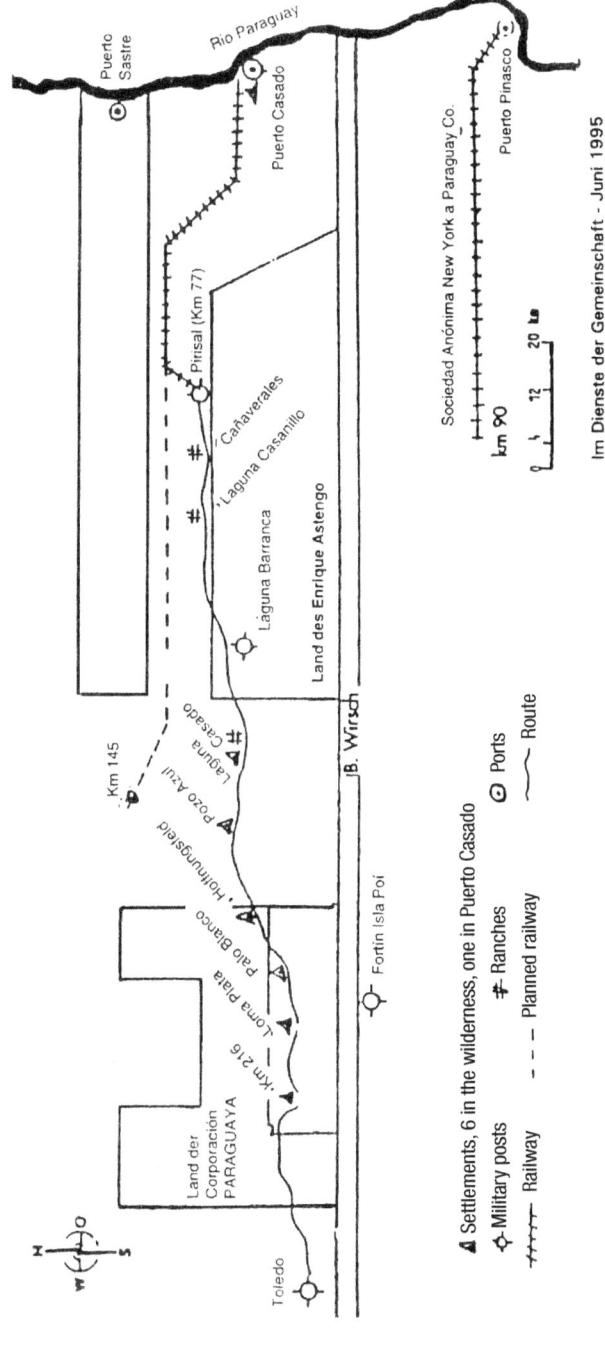

In one such incident, the wagon train came to a low-lying area filled with water. Because of the muddy ground it was decided to cross on foot. One ten-year old girl, however, was frightened to go into the water. A strong, young nineteen-year-old boy volunteered to carry her through the water. He took her up into his arms and started out. When he was knee deep in water he stumbled and both fell into the water. The young girl decided to walk on her own. Later it was discovered that this was not an accident; he had done this to help her overcome her fear of water, and it worked. [9]

These trips through the wilderness went very slowly and took many days and nights. They had to contend with every kind of weather. Each wagon was equipped with several tarps. Some of the wagons were covered and were protected from the rain and burning sun. Rain at night was especially uncomfortable. People had to huddle together in a covered wagon or be outside under a tarp to remain dry. Sleep was almost impossible. [10]

Finally, in April 1928, 16 months after the first settlers had arrived in Puerto Casado, the boundaries of the settlements were surveyed and the villages were laid out. The 1,248 survivors (of the 1,763 settlers that had originally come to Paraguay) could finally settle down on their own land.[11]

This is what the first villages looked like (Quiring, 1938)

---

[9] Ibid, pp. 8–9.
[10] Ibid, p. 9.
[11] See Martin W. Friesen, *Neue Heimat in der Chacowildnis* [A new home in the Chaco wilderness] (1978), chapter 10, 'Das große Sterben' [The great death], pp. 245–271.

The group received the title for their parcel of land (56,250 hectares, or 30 leguas) in September 1928. They named their new settlement Menno, after Menno Simons (1496–1561), one of the most important leaders of the early Anabaptist movement. After 1544 his followers were known as "Menniste," "Mennoniste," and finally "Mennonites." This name distinguished them as a peace-loving community, as opposed to some of the revolutionary Anabaptist groups of that time. [12]

In 1930 Fernheim Colony was established to the west of Menno Colony by German-speaking Russian Mennonite refugees. The arrival in 1932 of more refugees from Russia brought the population of this colony to 2,000.

In 1947 Neuland Colony, also consisting of refugees from the former Soviet Union, was established to the south of Fernheim Colony.

With this the immigration of the Mennonites into the Chaco came to an end. But what would happen now? This was a question to which no one really knew the answer. Several large Mennonite settlements had been established. Would they manage to survive? The future was uncertain. It was clear to many that the key to the success of the colonization project would be an adequate network of roads within the colonies and a road linking the colonies to markets. But how could this be accomplished when neither the country nor the Mennonites had the necessary resources? The transportation and road situation was the decisive concern since they had arrived; unfortunately, it would remain a significant drag on economic progress for many years.

---

[12] On the origin of this name and its meaning, see Heinhold Fast, "Wie sind die oberdeutschen 'Mennoniten' geworden?" [How did the South Germans become 'Mennonites'?] Mennonitische Geschichtsblätter 43/44 (1985/87), pp. 80–104.

3

Early Methods of Transportation among the Mennonites in the Chaco

The settlers in the Chaco were glad to finally live on their own piece of land. On the other hand, how could the development of the colonies progress when there were no roads and no means to build them? Good ideas were hard to come by, but no amount of complaining would help. Roads had to be cleared through the bush, with ax and shovel, connecting village to village. These could hardly be called real roads. The first road was constructed according to the principal of least resistance, going through grassy regions whenever possible. When it was impossible to avoid the thorny bush, large trees were skirted to save energy. The end result was long and very winding roads.

A typical span of oxen (Mennonite Life, January, 1950)

School field trip (Archiv Fernheim)

The lack of a transportation link and thus a means of bringing goods to market remained an especially serious challenge; it was for many years the greatest obstacle to the economic development of the Mennonite settlements.

In 1929 the Casado Company extended its narrow gauge railway up to Kilometer 145 To reach this end station (named "Fred Engen"), settlers from Loma Plata (Menno Colony) had to travel another 75 kilometers, those from Filadelfia (Fernheim Colony) 100 kilometers, and those from Neu-Halbstadt (Neuland) 135 kilometers. Some of Neuland's outlying villages were as far as 160 kilometers from the railway.

From the very beginning the three colonies lacked adequate means of transportation. Many farms did not have wagons; this was one of the first needs that had to be met and so several smithies were established for building wagons. Gradually the trail leading from the colonies to the railway station, Kilometer 145, was improved. The best route was found and trees were cut down, eliminating many curves. Potholes were filled, stretches that were uneven were leveled and the trail was widened so that in time one could properly speak of it as a road. Even so, the use of the road was still very dependent on good weather. During the rainy season it was almost impassable. [13]

---

[13] *Im Dienste der Gemeinschaft* (June 25, 1995), 12–15.

When the Russian Mennonites arrived in the Chaco in 1930, they were met at the railway station, Kilometer 145, by settlers from Menno, mostly in their ox carts, and taken to own new settlement. These Fernheim colonists had the good fortune that a network of "roads" had already been built by the Menno people and they were able to take advantage of this.

Eventually horses or mules replaced the oxen. This was a significant advance because horses could cover more than twice the distance per day that oxen could.

Another big step in the improvement of the roads came in 1942-1943 when MCC sent the Mennonites a grader. Since it did not have a motor, three span of oxen were hitched to it and the roads were planed and smoothed. This was progress.

In 1948 Menno Colony purchased its first Ford truck to be used for transport. In 1953 the first bulldozer arrived in the Chaco, a donation from North American Mennonites (see chapter 8). This was used to clear the bush and to build roads. More road-building equipment followed in 1954 with the arrival of Vern Buller (see chapter 9).

Menno Colony bought a second Ford truck, five-ton this time, in 1955. These trucks gradually eliminated the use of ox carts for the transport of goods.

On the way to church. K. Töws, Laubenheim (Quiring, 1936)

Setting out for Fred Engen (Railway station Km 145). H. Fehr, Laubenheim (Quiring, 1936)

What did it take in those early years to make the trip from the Mennonite settlements to Asunción? The ride to the train station could be completed in 4 days, depending on the means of transportation used and the weather. From there it took another day, or about 12 hours, by train to Puerto Casado. If all went well the trip to Asunción could be completed in one week. The same amount of time was needed for the return trip. Depending on the time spent in Asunción one could count on a return trip to take about three weeks. Towards the end of 1940 Abram W. Hiebert traveled to Asunción on behalf of Menno Colony. When he returned after three weeks he first received the sad news that in his absence one of his children had become ill, had died and had already been buried. [14]

The transportation system being what it was, the future of the Chaco colonies was by no means assured.

---

[14] *Ibid, p. 13*

4

Some Early Travel Report

Preacher Johann Teichgräf, **"A Preacher Travels to East Paraguay"** [15]

"On February 1, 1935, I began a trip to East Paraguay as a representative of the Fernheim Mennonite Church. The trip to Fred Engen Station (Kilometer 145) was made in five hours. We stayed there overnight. The next day, February 2, the train arrived at 10 o'clock in the morning, filled to overflowing with soldiers on leave (it was the time of the Chaco war). It took a great deal of effort to find a small place to sit among all the soldiers. There were five of us: the colony administrator, colony member W. Martens, two children of the P. Martens family living in Asuncion and the writer of these lines. We arrived in Puerto Casado after 12 hours, exhausted from the uncomfortable train ride in the overwhelming heat. We took our things to the hotel where we were given a room with three beds and soon were able to have a much-needed night's rest.

"We were not able to continue our trip until February 5. We took advantage of this time to explore the small port area.

"On February 5 at 11 o'clock at night we boarded the river steamboat Ciudad de Concepción and reached Asunción on February 7 at 6 o'clock in the morning. We had contacted Mr. Heinrichs, our representative, by telegram. He was there to give us a hearty welcome and accompany us through customs. On this occasion I was reminded of the narrow way and gate in Matthew 7:13-14. There was no other way into the city for any of the ship's passengers, only this one entrance. All other entrances were blocked off and locked. Our luggage was inspected, our visa had to be presented, and if all was in order we were free to go.

"In Asunción I was warmly welcomed by all of our people. During my stay I was able to serve seven times with a Word from God...

"Many people sent along greetings and well-wishes as I began my journey home on February 19. First I made a detour to Concepción and the

---

[15] *Mennoblatt, April 1935*

Riverboat Cuidad de Concepción (Mennonite Life, January 1950)

area surrounding Horqueta where a number of our people live. Here also I was the recipient of much loving kindness. What gave me special joy were the attentive listeners during the preaching of the Word….

"From here, accompanied by dear brothers and sisters, I went to the train station, and with many greetings to the colonists as we were known then, I arrived in Concepción on February 28.

"On March 1, again I boarded the riverboat, Ciudad de Concepción, and after the two-day boat, train and wagon ride, I returned home on March 8 in good health and found all my loved ones well in my home."

In the early years of the settlement there were many people in Fernheim who did not believe that there was a future in the Chaco. A number of the younger people moved to Asunción to look for opportunities to earn money. A new colony made up of Fernheim settlers, Neu-Hoffnung, was even established near Concepción.

An Impromptu Trip: The Opportunity to Travel (June, 1939)

"'Would you like to travel to East Paraguay to learn about the cultivation of ramie?' I was asked shortly after Pentecost by the Oberschulze (mayor) at the colony office. 'Yes,' I said, 'but doesn't your assistant, or our colony horticulturalist P. Esau, want to go?' He replied, 'I'm sure one of them would love to make the trip if the cotton harvest were not in full swing. And because the arrival of Dr. Fritz Kliewer from Germany has been delayed I am tied up at the high school. You know from Dr. Stranz's letter that he intends to travel to Europe soon. So if we intend to start cultivating ramie soon then we can hardly delay. So, please think about it.' I answered, 'All right, I will go.'

Roads in the Chaco

"I left the colony a few days later. I was with several others who were traveling to Asunción. The trip, made with a pair of strong mules, went well in the beautiful fall weather. We passed one load of cotton after another, for several kilometers. Then things began to change; now it started to become more difficult.

"The names Pozo Azul (Blue Well) and Palo Santo (named after the hardwood tree that grows here), will remain in the memory of every traveler that had to cross this stretch during the wet season. Not that these words will remind travelers of the well-maintained cattle stations; no, it is the roads that can drive a person mad.

"The land is low here but no longer sandy. Below the sand is a thick layer of impenetrable clay so standing water has to evaporate in the sun and wind. These are not as intense in June as they are in December; hence the terrible condition of the roads. Indeed, if these places could speak, what tales they would tell of animals being abused, of groaning and cursing, of praying, of crying! But they are silent, they remain mute. Anyone with eyes opened and a heart not yet turned to stone must feel sympathy for the humans and beasts condemned to travel at this time of the year.

"Pity the one who dares to leave home alone with a load of cotton! Even with two people it is a risky venture. If the wagon sinks, which happens often, and is up to the axle in mud, even the best pair of oxen or the most faithful horses will be unable to pull it free. If hitching a second team to the wagon doesn't work out there is nothing left to do but to roll the heavy bales off the wagon. Most of the time there are three or four bales, each weighing 250 kilos. Unloading them is one thing, but it is almost impossible for two men standing in muddy ground to load the bales again. Who knows how many injuries have been the result of the superhuman efforts

4. Some Early Travel Report

On the way to the railway (Quiring, 1938)

that are needed! … Occasionally the empty wagons are stuck so deep in the mud that the poor animals are unable to get them out.

"A teamster with a 'live load' is often the fortunate one. Sometimes his 'load' has to walk on its own four feet through the worst spots.

"Twenty-five kilometers short of our destination there is a four-kilometer stretch that is completely impassable for the wagonloads of cotton, although several have spent a whole day trying. The Casado administration gives permission by telephone to use another route.

By the Campfire

"Finally we are at the train station. It is amazing to see, while we all sit around the campfire, how the young men can keep their good humor and enjoy drinking their maté after the hard work of the day. The humor of the Germans seems to be indestructible. There is one funny joke after another, one anecdote more entertaining than the last, and riddle after riddle is shared as the young men try to outdo each other. Everyone is a cook, and the sweet potatoes are already baking in one campfire, while eggs and cracklings are frying over another.

"Eventually the gathering slowly disperses because the Southern Cross is almost horizontal in the dark southern sky, a sign that the witching hour

A rest stop at Hoffnungsfeld

is almost at hand. The ghostly, coffin-shaped mosquito nets are spread between two wagons. The tired drivers sleep under the nets and in their soft slumber are able to forget the trials of the day and gather strength for a new day that will surely demand all of one's energy. But woe to those who forgot their mosquito net or do not have one; in this region there is hardly a month without this plague of pests that we know so well in the colonies. A poor fellow without a net has to keep moving or sit by the smoke of the fire of palo santo wood.

"Soon only deep breathing can be heard as the tired animals graze on the grass and the sound of cowbells becomes our night music."

At Mr. Casado's

"Don José Casado, the old man, as well as his nephew, Don Carlos, are both at the port during this time. I am able to speak with them about several issues. The older man speaks German, since he studied in Germany.

"They are very interested in the plan to cultivate ramie in Fernheim. They also encourage us to grow sunflowers in order to produce oil. But soon we come to the delicate issue of roads in the Chaco. Mr. Casado blames the colonists: they are doing nothing to improve the roads. I try to

At the train station (1937)

find something to say in our defense: 'You see, Mr. Casado, our people are drowning in all of the work they have to do.' 'Well then,' Don José replies, 'your farmers should first work on the roads and then they would save a lot of time they now spend transporting their goods.

"I am interested in the railway, that is, the plan to extend it through the terrible swampy regions. Mr. Casado sketches a map on paper. According to his plan a spur of the railway would be built from Kilometer 160 past Hoffnungsfeld. The only problem is that there are no rails because at this time all steel throughout the world is being used for war needs. But it had been possible to buy rails for a stretch of railway; the rest would come, we had only to be patient.

"Un dia santo" (A Holy Day)

"The Toro has taken us aboard and soon the lights of the shore are behind us. Down in the hold of the ship there is music. On this steamboat there are always Paraguayan market women, the so-called "vendedoras" (sales women) who are allowed aboard at very good rates. They have sacks of oranges, tangerines, bananas, sausages, cheese, and other kinds of food. Everything is sold on the trip down: tomorrow they will disembark in Concepción to collect more wares to sell on their trip back. The large space that is usually used to transport cattle is decked out with flowers and

Perilous journey: 'Bear one another's burdens ...

other decorations. The women all wear bright silk dresses and wear their hair up, their lips and cheeks heavily rouged. This is what Paraguayans find attractive. They dance to Guaraní music and find partners among the ship's crew or among the other passengers.

"'What is this all about?' I ask one of the officers, who made a name for himself during the Chaco War and is the son-in-law of the current president, General Estigarribia. His replies: 'Es un dia santo, un cumpleaños!' ('It is a holy day; a birthday.')

The Japanese

"In the port of Concepción three Japanese join us; they become my cabin mates. They came by car from São Paulo, Brazil, and are traveling beyond Independencia to join a group of other Japanese. Since they speak Portuguese and we speak Spanish we can understand each other.

When they realize that we are German the two young men, very intelligent types, show us a book. On the cover is a picture of Bismarck. Between the peculiar block-shaped Japanese characters there are pictures of Moltke, Kaiser Wilhelm and others; we realize that the book is about German heroes. 'Bisamarko' and other German names are accompanied by lively gestures as are 'Hitera and Mussorini.' Apparently the Japanese cannot pronounce the 'l' and use the 'r' instead. We find this strange; it's exactly the opposite of what our children do!

When they are called to the dinner table with a wave and the cry, 'Tokyo,' one young man stands to attention and shouts 'Viva Berrin!' I try to teach him the right pronunciation, and with great effort he says, "Berrrrin, Hiterrrra and Mussorrrrini.' These Japanese quickly become everyone's favorite as we reach Asunción.

Asunción

"On Sunday afternoon the Toro slowly enters the Bay of Asunción. On shore our friends the Heinrichs and Fasts are already waving at us. We go through the passport checks and customs and soon the modern Ford brings us to the place where we will be staying. A little freshening up, a change of clothes, and we are on our way to the hotel 'Renania,' where the family of Dr. Fritz Kliewer arrived a few days earlier from Germany. The Kliewers naturally do not know that I too am in Asunción.

Meeting Again

"The surprise of my dear friend is great; his large eyes become even bigger when he sees me so unexpectedly after a five-year absence. 'Welcome, old Fritz!' and 'Ah, Nicholas, it's you!' those were most likely our first words. Who hasn't heard the saying that unexpected joy can cause sudden death, but at this moment death was the last thing on our minds. 'Gretchen, come meet my friend, Siemens from Fernheim,' he shouted and his voice carried all the way to the room where the family was staying. Soon the friendly lady from Berlin and I are shaking hands and a relationship is begun. Dr. Kliewer also proudly introduces me to his son.

An Outing

"Carrying on our lively conversation we reach the botanical gardens. The Mennonite youth of Asuncion have already arrived there by train ahead of us. Here on the lawn we have a celebration with songs, cake, and lemonade. We go to see the museum and the beautiful cemetery Recoleta and have a very pleasant afternoon.

Ramie

"On Monday I take the train 23 kilometers to Yuquyry station. From here I walk one kilometer and in the late afternoon I arrive at the home of Alfred Stranz. He welcomes me warmly into his home and serves me some refreshments. Mr. Stranz and his wife, along with their parents, are from Steiermark (Styria) and the familiar language sounds like music to my ears; when we lived in Siberia, during the war, there were Austrian prisoners of war who spoke this same language.

"We soon come to the topic of ramie. When it comes to ramie, Mr. Stranz is indefatigable. We tour his plantation, try out his home-made machine that removes the hard outer skin of the ramie leaves, and take many notes about the cultivation of ramie.

"I attempt to make an appointment with the Ministry of Agriculture to discuss ramie, to see if the government would be willing to assist the colonies in some way, for example, by helping them purchase seedlings. But this goes nowhere, for now at least, even though they strongly encourage the cultivation of ramie. Whenever I mention ramie, it is clear that people have a positive impression. Should cultivation be a success, this noble plant should lead to a bright future for Fernheim.

"I come to an agreement with Mr. Stranz and he promptly delivers 5,000 bulbs to the ship, all well packed in dirt.

"After completing our other business I leave Asunción that same week together with Mrs. Kliewer. Dr. Kliewer boards the ship in Rosario. He had gone ahead a few days earlier to visit our sister colony Friesland."

The attempt to grow ramie failed, as did many other similar ventures. But it showed that the Mennonites were trying very hard to overcome their economic stagnation. All of these failed ventures showed, as the above travel report above makes clear, that the lack of a transportation system – the time it took to travel, the crippling rainy season, the great expenditure of energy, the necessary layover in Casado – was an insurmountable barrier to a prosperous future. It is no surprise that under these circumstances many of the settlers, especially the leaders of the colonies, saw only a dark future ahead. No one dared to dream of a Trans-Chaco highway as we know it today.

5

MCC in Search of a Secure Future for Fellow Believers in Paraguay [17]

The Mennonite Central Committee (MCC) of North America was deeply concerned about the spiritual and physical well-being of their fellow believers in Paraguay. Serious thought was given as to how best to help them. For them to help "in the name of Christ" also meant economic assistance. Their ideal was to provide help so that recipients could help themselves. The desire to help their fellow believers improve their economic lot is clear from their attempt to help with the building of a textile factory. Cotton grows well in the Chaco, and is of good quality, but exports were severely hampered because of the lack of adequate roads. The brothers in MCC came up with the idea to build a textile factory ('Spinning and Weaving Plant') in the colonies. They promised to contribute both know-how and material assistance.

First attempt at plowing (1930)

---

[17] Cornelius J. Dyck and Frank Wiens, "Memorandum on the Establishment of a Spinning and Weaving Plant in the Chaco Mennonite Colonies, Paraguay." November 16, 1950.

Cornelius J. Dyck, MCC Director for South America, and Frank J. Wiens, made their way to South America in 1950 to explore the possibility.

They first visited the textile factory, Impresas Industrial Garcia, S.A., in Blumenau, Santa Catarina, Brazil. The director, Ernesto Stodienck, proved to be very amenable to answering the visitors' questions. The operations manager was Bernhard Enns, a Mennonite who had worked in the firm for 19 years. The factory employed 1,300 people and produced 450,000 to 500,000 square meters of fabric per month. The high quality spinning and weaving machines had been purchased from J.J. Rieter & Co. in Winterthur, Switzerland.

Since the representatives of the Swiss firm lived in Buenos Aires, Dyck and Wiens went there to gather more information. Mr. Stahel, chief of the firm in Buenos Aires, whose grandmother had belonged to the Swiss Anabaptists (Taufgesinnten), was very sympathetic and willing to help in every way he could. His readiness to help the Mennonites in the Chaco – he probably also smelled some business – was clear from his willingness to travel to the Chaco at his own expense to view the proposed site and give them

Plastering the house (1934)

Homemade seeders (1936)

a concrete proposal. The brothers from MCC requested a cost analysis for a factory with approximately 100 employees. The figure was US $241,316. This included the purchase of machines, transport and installation. In addition, the Mennonites would have to put up buildings, one 50 by 25 meters, the other 30 by 20 meters, and purchase a steam locomotive with 300 horsepower. Since a textile factory needs a lot of water this problem too would need to be addressed. Numerous wells would have to be dug and water tanks would need to be built.

The sale of the finished product in Paraguay in the form of fabric, thread, string and rope would not be a problem since there was a great need for these products and the demand was not being met.

It was MCC's plan to promote this project among wealthy men in the United States and Canada who would make this happen in partnership with the Mennonites in the Chaco. MCC, the "big brother" of the Mennonites in Paraguay, would support them with its blessing and advice for the undertaking.

Sawmill in Filadelfia (1937, Archiv Fernheim)

Regrettably, this promising project, as well as others that are not named here, never materialized. The reasons for this are not clear. It is possible that it failed because it was impossible to secure the necessary water supply. Even so, MCC never gave up looking for new ways to help the Mennonites in the Chaco. Over and over again the essential need for a road – a Trans Chaco highway – connecting the Mennonites with Asunción was recognized. Did one dare to dream for this?

6

A Memorandum [18]

Dr. J. Winfield Fretz, Professor of Sociology and Economics at Bethel College, North Newton, Kansas, came to Paraguay to study the economic and social situation of the Mennonites in Paraguay. He made a thorough study of the issues. His report laid out the situation of the Mennonites in great detail. For the sake of an accurate comparison, he included the amounts of money that MCC had invested in settling the Russian Mennonites in the Chaco. It was almost US $2 million, a very large sum at the time.

On the one hand, Fretz was deeply impressed with what the Mennonites had accomplished, even though they had had help from outside. They had their own telephone system, their own electricity, oil presses, cotton gins, two foundries, and their own machine shops in which seeders and threshing machines were built. The Mennonites had proved that it was possible to live in the Chaco and that more than enough food could be produced. The spiritual, social and cultural life, as well as the Colony administration had been well organized, and future development could confidently be expected.

However there was the big BUT. The situation was extremely difficult. The living standards were poor. Agricultural produce could not be delivered because the market was far away and there were no roads. The Mennonites also needed industries on a larger scale – a textile factory – but then again a connection to Asuncion was needed for this to be a success. Fretz proposed several options: building a railway to the colonies, using freight planes, or building roads from the colonies to Concepción, with connections by river boat to Asunción.

After thoroughly laying out the situation Fretz cautiously asked the director of Point IV if the development of the Chaco would be of interest to them and could be added to their program. He pointed out that

---

[18] *J. Winfried Fretz and Albien W. Patterson, Director of STICA and coordinator for Point IV in Paraguay. Asunción, August 24, 1951.*

MCC and the US government had the same goals: economic development aid. The development of the Chaco would surely be of interest to the Paraguayan government and would not only be of value to the Mennonites, the whole country would benefit from it.

In fact, if Point IV (for more on the history and goals of 'Point IV', see chapter 18) was seriously interested in building a road from the colonies to Concepción, Fretz suggested a committee should be formed, consisting of representatives from Point IV, the three Mennonite colonies in the Chaco and MCC, that would investigate the possibility of building a road.

A committee did not materialize at this time but the contacts made with Point IV were fundamental for the eventual construction of the Trans-Chaco Highway. The seed of a partnership had been planted; it was nurtured and eventually grew. When in 1961 the highway to the colonies was near completion, Fretz wrote that he had not thought it possible in 1951 that within 10 years the road would become a reality. A dream would become reality. [19]

---

[19] "The Trans-Chaco Road," *Christian Living* (February 1960), p. 4.

7

The Critical Situation of the Mennonites in the Chaco: *"To Be or Not to Be"*

In the mid-1950s the Mennonite colonies in the Chaco were in the midst of a crisis. Peter P. Klassen wrote: "Even in 1950 a number of circumstances in all the colonies led to an emigration movement that temporarily put into question the existence of some of the colonies. Depression and discouragement spread like a disease that was rapidly transmitted from one colony to another...." [20] What caused this critical situation? "The main cause of the crisis and the resulting emigration was the great difficulty in getting ahead economically...." [21]

Many too became ill because they were unaccustomed to the tropical climate. Repeated years of drought and plagues of locusts and other pests greatly reduced the crops. But the fundamental problem was the marketing of their products, which was not profitable because of the great distance from the colonies to the market. The attempt to build factories in the Chaco to process products like cotton and peanuts had failed. Many settlers in the Chaco saw no future and left the country for Brazil, Argentina, Canada or Germany to make a new life for themselves. A mass exodus began. Klassen concluded: "For the Mennonite colonies in Paraguay it was truly a matter of to be or not to be. Emigration put their being into question." [22] The greatest number of emigrants were from Neuland and the fewest from Menno. Between 1952 and 1957, 1,224 people left Neuland Colony. At the time the colony was established Neuland had had a population of 2,256. [23]

Heinz Braun, viewing the food situation, wrote in the Neuland anniversary book: "A catastrophe threatens." [24] Braun continues:

---

[20] Peter P. Klassen, *Die Mennoniten in Paraguay: Reich Gottes und Reich dieser Welt* (The Mennonites in Paraguay: The Kingdom of God and the Kingdom of this World) (1988), pp. 154–155.
[21] Ibid., p. 155.
[22] Ibid., p. 154.
[23] Walter Regehr, *25 Jahre Kolonie Neuland (1947–1972): Eine Gedenkschrift zum fünfundzwanzigjährigen Jubiläum* (1972), p. 19.
[24] Ibid., p. 24.

"When the colony was founded, there were only two roads from the neighboring colonies to the new settlement. These were overgrown trails from the Chaco War. The one led from Filadelfia through Number 5 and Carayá to Landskrone. From here it branched off past Lichtenau-Neuendorf to Neu-Halbstadt and followed the grassland region to Schönhorst and Platanillo. The other branch led to Einlage-Altenau-Steinfeld and further past Arce to the Pilcomayo River. The other road went from Isla Poí near Menno to Boquerón past Tiege and then reconnected to the road going to Arce."

"There were four large high grasslands (wooded savannahs) extending from west to east through the colony's land. The villages were established along these savannahs as was the vehicle traffic. It took a lot of time to travel these winding roads, and the sandy soil made travel difficult."

"As soon as possible the villages were connected with wider and straighter roads to the centrally located Neu-Halbstadt. Often the only way to determine where to build the roads was to light a large fire at the destination. On a cloudy night, the reflection of the fire on the low hanging clouds lit up twenty kilometers or more in every direction. Initially a trail one meter wide was cut through the bush. If it led successfully to the intended destination, the trail was cleared into a broader, useable road. This is how all of the roads in the colony were constructed. After 1956 they were cleared with a bulldozer (see 'Vern Bu-

At the village well in Friedensheim, Neuland (Regehr, 1972)

A "roof" above one's head, Neuland (Regehr, 1972)

ller,' chapter 9) and built up and leveled with a motorized grader so that it was possible to drive on sooner after rain. This first road-building equipment was a gift from MCC to the colonies. Communication was also very difficult in the beginning because the most distant villages were 40 kilometers from the center of the colony" [25]

Braun also reports of great loss of goods due to how long it took to transport. Along the way, goods often had to be reloaded. On one occasion 300 sacks of flour were stacked on grasshopper poison during the process of reloading and became unfit for consumption. [26]

Had the Trans-Chaco highway not been built, this colony might have been disbanded completely. The completion of the Trans-Chaco highway in 1961 did not solve every problem but it contributed considerably to economic progress and the improvement of living standards in the colonies.

---

[25] Ibid., pp. 29–30.
[26] See ibid., pp. 24–25.

A beginning has been made; what will happen next? (Regehr, 1972)

8

The Inspiring Example of Harry Harder

The first bulldozer to be used in the Chaco was brought to Paraguay in 1952 by an American Mennonite, Harry Harder. Harder called this venture a "Mennonite Men project" or "Brotherhood project." Here is his story in his own words:

"In 1950 Dr. J. R. Schmidt spoke in a local church about the poor road conditions in Paraguay and the urgent need for bulldozers to build roads. He also showed pictures of the living conditions there."

"On June 13, 1950, after the Northern District Conference in Mountain Lake, Minnesota, a group of men met and discussed the conditions among the Mennonite refugees in their colonies in Paraguay. This group of men agreed to raise money to buy a bulldozer and send it to Paraguay to build roads in the five Mennonite colonies (Volendam, Friesland, Menno, Fernheim, and Neuland). Dr. John R. Schmidt, a physician, had already talked to me a number of times about the need for a bulldozer to build roads for the Mennonites in Paraguay. Since I had many years' experience in road building and knew how to repair the equipment, he thought that I was the right person to go to Paraguay with the bulldozer and train local people in road building and equipment maintenance."

"A year later, in 1951, at the next annual Northern District Conference, enough money had been raised to buy a bulldozer. Henry M. Harder, the chairman of the Northern District men's group, and I met with the MCC executive committee in Chicago on June 28, 1951. We worked out an agreement whereby MCC personnel would help with transporting the equipment to Paraguay and with supervision of the work there. I remember a committee member asking me, "How can you spread the Gospel with a bulldozer?" After the meeting P. C. Hiebert, H. M. Harder and I traveled to the Caterpillar factory in Peoria, Illinois, and placed an order for a D7 bulldozer. The bulldozer left the factory in October 1951, and arrived in Asunción in March 1952. The Caterpillar dealer in Asuncion was legally entitled to a commission on the sale of the bulldozer but he refused to accept it. He praised the fact that the American Mennonites would do something like this for their fellow believers in Paraguay.

"On April 14, 1952, I said goodbye to my wife and children and flew to Paraguay. When I arrived at the MCC home in Asunción the bulldozer was already standing there. My first job was to grade a soccer field at a vocational school. Then I drove the bulldozer to the river port and loaded it and the blade grader on to the boat to ship these machines to Mbopicuá.

"I followed the next day on another riverboat, arriving at midnight. The boat stopped in the middle of the river and two Mennonite men from Volendam, whom I didn't know, picked me up in a rowboat.

"The next day several of the colony's leaders came on horseback to visit me in Mbopicuá. They had brought along an extra horse for me, so we rode through the areas where they wanted a road built. I rode for a while, but finally I dismounted and led the horse; I felt safer that way.

"The only road from Volendam to the river port, Mbopicuá, ran along an old railway track. The rails were gone but some of the ties were still there. That made for a very bumpy ride. We built a new road alongside the former railway. We also dug several water holes for cattle and one for a sawmill. While we were doing this, I trained two Mennonites from Volendam and one from the Chaco to use the road-building machines. The biggest problem we faced during this time were the many rains. Many days we could not work at all. During the week we lived in a trailer. Twice a week provisions were brought to us. On the weekend we went to Village No. 5 in Volendam Colony; MCC had a house there. Mrs. Klassen lived in the house across the street and brought me my meals. Sometimes I went to the hospital to eat.

"We had a lot of interesting experiences while working here. For example, we encountered many coral and rattlesnakes.

"One day the spring of the starter switch broke. There was nothing like it to be found in Volendam. It occurred to me that a knitting needle could be used to make one. I asked one of the Mennonite women if she had one. She had two and gave one of them to me. I wound the needle around a wooden shaft a quarter-inch thick and it made a nice spring. I installed it and it worked as long as I can remember.

"In the time spent working in Volendam I had to travel to Asunción quite often. The trip had to be made by boat. Unfortunately one never knew when the ship might come. There were always others, like me, who were waiting for the boat. Once we sat by the shore, waiting, till late at night. It was cold and very windy. Finally we found some branches and made a fire to keep us warm. After a while we grew tired and lay down to sleep. One person had to stay awake, ready to hail the boat with a kerosene lantern, should it finally arrive to pick us up.

"After a few months the road was finished and we moved on to Rosario to build a road between it and Friesland. The Paraguayan children from the town brought us armfuls of fruit and vegetables every day.

"One morning we found a dead horse where we wanted to build the road. I told one of the men to dig it a hole with the bulldozer and bury the horse. The next day the owner of the horse came and accused us of killing the horse. He went to the police, which caused us some trouble. So I went to talk to Oberschulze Wieler, told him the story, and he took care of the situation.

"On weekends I went to Friesland. One Sunday when I arrived at my house I found that it had been visited by a horse; it had left behind a big pile of manure on my bed.

"From Rosario to Friesland is about 36 kilometers (22 miles). The closer one gets to the colony, the higher and harder the ground is. In some places our bulldozer could not break it up. The Ministerio de Obras Públicas (Ministry of Public Works) came to our rescue with a high hoe that was able to break up the hard soil.

"The time came for me to return to the United States. [Harder arrived home on December 24, 1952]. By now, the two men from East Paraguay and the one from the Chaco had been well trained and did good work. They continued working in Friesland for several months. Then the bulldozer was shipped via Puerto Rosario and Puerto Casado and taken to the Mennonites in the Chaco to clear the bush and build roads. Later Menno Colony bought the bulldozer: Jacob Dyck, from Menno, who was one of those first three men I trained, operated it till the 1970s. Nobody has ever counted how many hours that bulldozer worked."

It was this bulldozer, according to Harder, that led the Chaco Mennonites to think that it would be possible to build a road from the Chaco colonies directly to Asunción, and from the colonies further on to Bolivia. In 1952, however, this was still only a wishful thought, a utopian dream.

Further details to the report by Harry Harder can be found in a letter from Henry M. Harder about the bulldozer project. This is the Henry Harder mentioned above, the leader of the Mennonite men's group of Mountain Lake, Minnesota. He writes:

"There were people who said that this would never work. Raising money for the purchase of a bulldozer was an act of faith. Hundreds of letters were written and many church members were approached personally. [76] In many congregations men's groups were formed and many became enthusiastic about the project. At the next annual district conference meeting, in Munich, North Dakota, June 1951, the men met again. In the meantime the group had become a Men's Association of the conference. A total of $9,556.04 had already been raised. The information was shared with the conference assembly. It brought to mind Genesis 1:1, 'In the beginning God.' God was the source and origin of the work. God was involved in the plans and the organization. We were also reminded of the words of the Apostle Paul, 'God has opened a door for me' (1 Cor. 16:9, 2 Cor. 2:12). We had to take advantage of this open door.

"After the business meeting two brethren each gave $2,500 toward the purchase of a bulldozer.

"Harry Harder came forward to volunteer his time from April 14 through December 24, 1952. His round-trip fare was paid by the Northern District Conference. The men's group purchased a large crate of good-quality tools. In the end the whole project cost $18,468.94. There was $1,131.10 left over in the account." [27]

A chain of actions can be discerned in the accounts given above. Dr. John Schmidt, an American physician, served among the Mennonites in the Chaco, under very primitive living conditions. Beginning at the end of 1950, he dedicated himself to a new task, those in Paraguay who suffer from leprosy. This was the start of the Km 81 hospital, supported by the Mennonites in Paraguay. The suffering of so many people in Paraguay made a deep impression on Dr. Schmidt. Even though the Mennonites in Paraguay were themselves still very poor, they were ready to help those

---

[27] H. M. Harder, "Northern District Brotherhood," *Mennonite Life* (October 1954), pp. 170–171.

who were even poorer. This led Dr. Schmidt to think that the Mennonites could do far more for the people of the country, if conditions were to permit them to do so. They needed to be helped so that they would be in a position to help others. Communications and export markets were two of their biggest problems. As long as there were no roads, however, there was no hope that the economic climate could be improved. The same was true of the Mennonite colonies in East Paraguay, Friesland and Volendam.

A good road from these colonies to the ports along the Paraguay River – distances that were not insurmountable – would surely mean a great deal for the development of Friesland and Volendam.

With these concerns in his heart, Dr. Schmidt visited his congregations in the United States. The economic situation in his homeland was in stark contrast to the poverty he had seen in Paraguay. In his visits to individual congregations and at Mennonite conferences and assemblies, he returned again and again to this theme. The slides of Paraguay he had brought with him illustrate his point. On top of this, Dr. Schmidt also had conversations with ordinary individuals and impressed on them the need to use the resources God has given them to help the people of Paraguay, so that they could help others in turn. This is the way of life, after all, that has distinguished Mennonites for centuries: each person helps another, so that this person too can help a neighbor. In this way a chain reaction of good deeds is set in motion.

These notions were taken up by the leaders of the Mennonite Conference, by Harry Harder and others. They too sought out others to talk to, and a project was born. The Mennonites who would benefit from this project couldn't yet imagine that this project would be the catalyst for other much larger projects. No one yet knew this. The important point was that a project had been initiated with a purpose– to help brothers and sisters in need and through them to help others also.

The example of Harry Harder showed how the initiative of one individual and enthusiasm of a single congregation could inspire good works. "Do not neglect to do good and to share what you have, for such sacrifices are pleasing to God" (Hebrews 13:16). Doing good is contagious; that was certainly true of this project. The first project was barely completed, and already the opportunity presented itself for another, the road-building project of Vern Buller, another step towards the initiation of the Trans-Chaco highway.

9

Vern Buller – A "Modern Prophet"

> *"Every valley shall be raised up and every hill made low."*
> *Isaiah 40.4*

This is the text that C. L. Graber applied to the work Vern Buller and his team did building roads among the Mennonite colonies in the Paraguayan Chaco. [28]

Buller was 'one who prepares the way' in the truest sense of the word. Frank Wiens referred to him as a "modern prophet" alluding to the words of Isaiah cited above and the example of John the Baptist. [29] Wiens offers no further explanation of what his understanding of modern prophet might be. Maybe Wiens simply wanted to say that Vern Buller represented something very special for the Mennonites in Paraguay, just as the prophets with their own distinct acts had been extraordinary people in their time.

Again the story begins at a Mennonite conference (Northern District), this time in Bloomfield, Montana, on June 11, 1953. Vern Buller attended this conference and made a proposal to those present that many must have thought utopian. He volunteered to take his road-building machines to the Mennonites in the Chaco of Paraguay to build the roads that were so necessary for their economic development. He proposed to put the following machines at the disposal of this project.

1 TD18 International bulldozer

1 Adams elevating grader

1 Caterpillar no. 60 14-foot road grader

1 LeTourneau self-loading four-wheel drive scraper

1 Jeep

---
[28] H. M. Harder, "Northern District Brotherhood," *Mennonite Life* (October 1954), pp. 170–171.
[29] Frank J. Wiens, "Annual Report on the South American Program" (1959).

In addition he was prepared to provide the necessary tools and parts, valued at $20,000, at his own expense.

At the businessmen's association meeting during the conference the following resolution was passed:

"That we, with thankful hearts, accept the generous offer of Vern Buller of Richey, Montana, to take his International TD18 crawler-type tractor with bulldozer blade, Le Tourneau 8–10 cubic yard self-loading four-wheel drive scraper and Caterpillar No. 60 grader with 14-foot blade to Paraguay to help our Mennonite brethren with the building of roads; and to accept his offer to donate two year's time to operate the same. Also, that we accept the offer of Isaac P. Tieszen of the Tieszen Clinic, Marion, South Dakota, for underwriting the freight of the above-mentioned equipment to Paraguay, while giving opportunity for others to contribute also toward payment of this freight." [30]

The businessmen's association agreed to assume the round-trip transportation costs of the Vern Buller family. This would cost approximately $3,000. [31]

On April 5, 1954, more than 40 tons of machinery left New Orleans by boat and arrived in Asunción on August 16, 1954.

MCC was asked to take on the cost of shipping these machines to Paraguay. Buller offered to go to Paraguay as a Christian voluntary service worker under MCC, together with his wife and three children, to supervise the road building, and to train local people in the techniques of road building and in the maintenance and operation of the road-building machinery. Heavy machinery like this was unknown in Paraguay at the time. All of the machines were to remain in the Chaco when this specific project was completed, for use in building additional roads. [32]

As soon as he arrived in the Chaco, Buller went to work. The most important road, from Kilometer 145 to Loma Plata–Filadelfia–Neu-Halbstadt, was completed already in the second half of the year 1955. Altogether about 135 kilometers of road were built in less than one year. The road building was then continued in the colonies.

A few years earlier MCC had sent the Mennonites a D7 Caterpillar bulldozer and a grader for road building (see chapter 8). Buller and his wor-

---

[30] H. M. Harder, "Northern District Brotherhood," *Mennonite Life* (October 1954), p. 171.
[31] Ibid.
[32] Letter from W. T. Snyder to Dr. Willfried Mauck, April 5, 1954.

kers were able to use these in their work. MCC flew five Pax men to the Chaco to help with the work; they had experience with heavy machinery while working on a Le Tourneau project in the jungle of Peru.

Buller first built a road from the Chaco colonies to End Station (Kilometer 145), a distance of 75 kilometers. This was finished in February of 1955. The next step was to connect the three colony centers, Loma Plata, Filadelfia and Neu-Halbstadt, with a good road. The road from Hofnungsfeld to Filadelfia was finished by July 1, 1955.

What these roads meant for transportation within the colonies is clear from the following examples. A horse-drawn wagon with a load of 500 to 1,000 kilograms took 30 hours on average to reach End Station (one way). On the new road a 3-ton truck could make the round trip in 10 hours. The stretch between Filadelfia and Neu-Halbstadt (32 kilometers) could be traveled in 40 minutes by jeep. Before, the same vehicle had taken an hour and 45 minutes on the same stretch. A new era for transportation in the Mennonite colonies in the Chaco had begun. Hope began to grow among the settlers.

Even before the road to End Station had been completed, Fernheim colony purchased a 16.5-ton steam engine. But how to bring this monster to Filadelfia? Buller had an idea. He built a trailer of the right size and the steam engine was loaded on it. A Farmall M tractor made the 15-hour trip to bring this load to Filadelfia. The trailer later was modified for transport and was able to carry 10 tons of freight from Filadelfia to End Station in one day.

C. L. Graber suggested that the new road to the train station be named "Highway of Peace" (Pax Highway). [83] A modern-day practical prophet had, with the help of others, made plain the uneven ground, because "the glory of the Lord shall be revealed and all people will see it together" (Isaiah 40:5).

The construction of these roads made a deep impression on the national government and had far-reaching consequences for the development of the Chaco and especially for the Trans-Chaco highway project:

1. Transportation within the colonies was greatly improved and made much easier. Travel to End Station was also much easier and quicker, and greatly enhanced contact with the outside world. The difference

between using oxen, then horses, finally automobiles was great.

2. The new roads gave the Mennonites in the Chaco new enthusiasm and determination in their critical situation. They had hope for a better future and were encouraged to persevere.

3. The roads built under Vern Buller's leadership made the building of a road from the Chaco colonies to Asunción a realistic possibility. He had demonstrated that roads in the Chaco could be built quickly and economically. The plans for the building of the Trans-Chaco highway began to take concrete form. National and international interest was aroused in the project to build the Trans-Chaco highway and in the development of the Chaco.

4. The road construction work of Vern Buller was a practical example of brother helping brother and loving one's neighbor. This mission illustrates how material wealth can be used to improve the lot of others and be of great service to many. It was an example of development assistance motivated by Christian love.

The Mennonites in the Chaco, and not only the Mennonites, are still today beneficiaries of this selfless, exemplary Christian deed. It is an invitation for all to imitate. We Mennonites in Paraguay do well to remind ourselves of this. Deeds really do speak louder than words.

10

It Began with a Stomach Operation

Dr. Gerhard Dollinger[33] is one of the most important doctors in the history of Mennonites in Paraguay. He was born in 1914 in Schwabia, Germany. During the Second World War he was captured by the Americans. He was not a Mennonite, but he came into contact with the Mennonites and with MCC, and because of this connection he ended up in Fernheim, Chaco, in 1951 as a missionary doctor. The Mennonites desperately needed a doctor, and his skills and ease with people soon won him the hearts of all of the Fernheimers. He remained among the Mennonites in Paraguay for 13 years. He was an excellent story-teller, with a flare for the dramatic. He would later describe many of his experiences in the Chaco in his book. [34] What follows is a summary of one of his chapters. It is an uplifting story, vividly told, about Vern Buller by the German doctor in the Chaco It describes the events that are the background to Vern Buller's presence in Paraguay.

Dr. Dollinger begins by describing the challenges confronting a doctor in the Chaco: "We faced constant challenges providing adequate care in our little hospital in the bush. Sometimes the care packages from Germany were delayed for months at a time, or a certain item that we badly needed was nowhere to be had in the entire country. One day we badly needed an anesthetic. We really should operate, with or without the anesthetic. What to do? It is possible to perform many operations using only a local anesthetic, freezing the area in question. But at home in Germany I had never performed a surgical invasion of the stomach cavity using only a local anesthetic. No one thought it possible because a patient who was not unconscious would naturally push the intestines out of the cavity and it would be impossible to operate. I had to come up with another plan, therefore, to deal with acute cases that could not be postponed until a shipment of anesthetic had finally arrived".

---

[33] *Lexikon der Mennoniten in Paraguay (Asunción, Paraguay: Verein für Geschichte und Kultur der Mennoniten in Paraguay, 2009), pp. 111–112.*
[34] *Gerhard Dollinger, Das Paradies in der grünen Hölle: Was ein Landarzt erzählt (Stuttgart: J. F. Steinkopf Verlag, 1993), pp. 87–92.*

10. It All Began with a Stomach Operation

What could Dr. Dollinger do? An opportunity presented itself when a man who loved to sing came to him for an operation. Dr. Dollinger asked him, half in jest and half in earnest, whether he would be willing to sing during the operation. The patient agreed to the proposal provided that the singing would not distract the doctor during the operation. Dr. Dollinger describes the operation: "I thought of a few songs and assigned the four parts: the patient would sing the tenor part, I the bass, the operating room nurse the soprano, and my wife the alto. I froze the patient's stomach and, when I was ready to begin cutting, we all four began to sing:

'O Liebe, gold'ner Sonnenschein

fürs arme Menschenherz

Strahlst du nur hell in mich hinein

versüßt is jeder Schmerz.'

(O love, like golden sunshine on our poor hearts; when you shine brightly on me, every sorrow is transformed)

"We sang every verse of this song, then the next song, and so on, until I had sewn up the patient. When I said 'done' the patient, who had sung along the whole time and at the top of his voice, said he had felt absolutely nothing".

Dr. Dollinger's new operating technique became the talk of the colony and beyond. As the doctor notes, from now on every patient wanted an operation with four-part harmony. One patient, who couldn't sing but knew how to play the mouth organ, wanted to play it during the operation. He was allowed to do so. It did not take long for his operating technique to become known beyond the borders of Paraguay. One day an American reporter visited Dr. Dollinger in the Chaco bush in order to see for herself whether it was possible to operate on someone who was singing. She could understand that a nurse or even a doctor would be able to sing during an operation. But that a patient could sing while a doctor was operating on his stomach – this she had to see to believe. Both doctor and patient were willing to let her watch and so she was able to see this happen with her own eyes.

When she returned to the US, she wrote a story for Reader's Digest, a magazine read around the world, describing what she had seen in a remote hospital in the Paraguayan Chaco. Dr. Dollinger's new operating method became famous around the world and he began to receive hundreds of letters. One correspondent even wrote from a meteorological observation station in the Antarctic.

One day a rich American showed up at the clinic. He had read the story in Reader's Digest, he told the doctor, and "I have two ruptured hernias and have come all the way from Montana [USA], near the Canadian border, in order to be operated by you. With singing, please. But I'm a very busy man and don't have a lot of time. I won't stay to have the stitches taken out – my family doctor at home can do that."

The American had to wait two days for his operation, days he spent visiting the colonies. He noticed the marginal conditions in the colonies: the lack of water and above all the lack of roads with the closest market 500 kilometers away. How could anyone survive here? Dr. Dollinger describes the operation in his inimitable style:

"We operated on Vern Buller, after we had agreed on a few songs that he knew in English and we in German. So we sang in four parts in two languages. When I called out 'Finished,' he replied, 'What? Really? I didn't feel a single stitch! So you're not a liar after all and it was worthwhile that I came all the way from Montana to your little bush hospital.'

"When we said goodbye to each other, he said, 'You'll hear from me again.'"

The man was Vern Buller from Montana, US, a wealthy farmer. Days, weeks and months went by. Then, after a long time, Dollinger heard that Vern Buller was on his way back to Paraguay, but not in order to have another operation. He was coming with his family and his road-building machines, in order to build much-needed roads in the Chaco. Vern Buller explained to Dr. Dollinger why he had come:

"When I came here and looked around a bit, I thought to myself: these settlers will never be able to make any progress so long as there are no good roads and no connection to the outside world. Why don't you come here and build roads for them? At first I looked for a government agency that would fund my idea – development aid or something similar. But all of my attempts to find funding failed. Nobody wanted to finance this project. Then I thought: that German doctor down there left his home, left everything behind and, completely on his own and without receiving any money from his home country, he went into the bush. Until now you've only ever worked for yourself. Isn't it time that you did something for the Lord? If no one wants to support you, go on your own, you can afford it after all. So I leased out my farms for two years, loaded my road-building business on a ship, and flew out here with my wife and three children. The children can go to school here; it won't hurt them to learn German."¹

When the project in the Chaco was finished, Buller donated his road construction machinery to the Mennonites so that they could continue building roads. The Jeep, however, was given to Dr. Dollinger to help him in his work at the hospital.

In this story Dr. Dollinger highlights the special role played by Vern Buller. Buller came to Paraguay on his own initiative and built the roads connecting the Chaco colonies, roads that were so badly needed. In any case, it appears that his unusual operating technique is the true origin of Buller's actions; Dollinger suggests that Buller first came to the Chaco because he had read about Dr. Dollinger in Reader's Digest. Buller himself nowhere makes this connection explicit. In response to my repeated requests, he has informed me via Edgar Stoesz that the story about the operation is substantially correct, but that his call to go to Paraguay to build roads there came directly from God. More about this in the next chapter.

11

Vern Buller Looks Back

I had completed the last chapter when I received the following very detailed, informative report and many photos from Vern Buller. Some of it repeats a number of things that appear above and not all of his report is germane to the topic of this book. Nevertheless, I include it here, slightly abbreviated, because he does include information and thoughts that should provoke reflection and motivate others. He writes in retrospect after forty years:

"I, Vern Cecil Buller, was born May 29, 1918, to Isaac and Yettie Buller of Richey, Montana. I was raised on a farm and learned the basics of life – how to raise crops of wheat, oats, and barley. I was very inquisitive from early childhood about how things were made and what they could do, especially things with moving parts. Because of the farm work, and being the oldest of seven children, my father taught me at an early age to operate tractors and other farm equipment. By the age of eight I had to stay home from school to help my father and was often discouraged to find that I was behind the other students in my class. I never finished the seventh grade and did not have any further schooling other than self-learning, asking questions and taking things apart and putting them back together again. I always felt that there was no such thing as 'It can't be done.'

"As far as church life is concerned, I had very little of it until I became a teenager. It was then my desire to go to church like I saw others do. I would ask for the family car and my brother and I started attending church occasionally on our own.

"My family and I moved to South Dakota when I was eighteen years old. At the age of twenty-one I had the urge to start my own life and was permitted to move back to Montana to take over the family farm. After returning to Montana I started attending church regularly because of my friends. During a revival meeting in June 1940, I was moved to go forward and accept Christ as my Savior and Lord. Later in September 1940, I was baptized and became a member of the Bethlehem Mennonite Church of Bloomfield, Montana, where I am still a member.

"After returning to Montana I met Violet Richert, a girl that I had gone to school with some years earlier. I found her to be a beautiful young lady. She was the daughter of Ben and Susie Richert. We were married on December 28, 1941, and continued to live on the farm except for the six years we spent in Paraguay.

"I love to help people. After World War II we heard through the Mennonite Church about being able to have displaced people live with us. We contacted MCC and asked for a family and were assigned a Ukrainian couple with one daughter. In January 1950, they came to live with us in our home for one year. The agreement when we took the family in was that we would be responsible for their living expenses so they would not be a burden to the government or MCC. We learned to like these people very much. We could work with them and they ate at our table like our own family. During a layover in Chicago on their way to our place, the family found out they had relatives in the Chicago area. After corresponding with them, the relatives coaxed them to join them, promising they would be able to find jobs there. After about five months the government permitted them to join their relatives. We missed them very much but understood their feelings of wanting to be close to their own people. We kept in touch with them for many years.

"Through this experience we felt that there was more we should do, but what? In June 1952 the Northern District Conference (affiliated with the General Conference Mennonite Church) was held at Mountain Lake, Minnesota. Dr. John Schmidt, the doctor who started KM 81 in Paraguay, was also attending the conference. He made a plea to the men of the Northern District to buy a bulldozer and donate it to the colonies in Paraguay. He wanted to send someone who could teach them to operate and maintain it. The men decided to take this on as a project. A delegate from my home church was at the conference and approached me about volunteering to go, but Harry Harder from Mountain Lake had already volunteered. The thought of doing something like this became a challenge for me but I still didn't know what.

"In April 1953, while I was out on my own bulldozer seeding and farming and alone with my thoughts, I believe that God sent an angel to me.

Through the presence of the angel, God revealed to me that I should give my bulldozer and go myself to Paraguay. The first time this happened it seemed more like a dream and I pondered how I would accomplish this task. It happened again and after the third and fourth time it became clear to me that God was asking me to go. For some reason that experience was laid aside until the second week of June 1953, when the conference met in our church. Harry Harder, who had taken up the challenge the year before to take the bulldozer to Paraguay, was at the conference and showed pictures of the project. At the close of the presentation he said they could use more bulldozers and that awakened the experience I had in the wheat field earlier in the spring. That evening after we returned home from the service I could not sleep. I kept thinking about what had been said and the need of the colonies in Paraguay. The next morning when we drove to church for the conference we entered the church yard at the same time as the president of the men's organization, H. M. Harder. I told him I wanted to give my bulldozer and myself to the three colonies of the Chaco for two years.

"Mr. Harder asked me to present this news to the men during the Mennonite Men's meeting that afternoon. When I did, the response was positive and they voted to accept the offer. Dr. Isaac Tieszen of Marion, South Dakota, then said that he felt this project should begin immediately and offered to underwrite the freight and airfare for the Buller family. Since the bulldozer was privately owned we were sure it would be hard to get through customs, so we donated it to MCC. They, in turn, could give it to the colonies. This is how MCC became involved and how we became volunteer workers for MCC.

"Because this all took place in June 1953, the summer work and harvest kept the project from progressing except for correspondence to get it on its way. I started making plans and thought that the bulldozer was probably getting a little too old. I shopped around for a newer one and was offered a newer model. When I got the bulldozer home I took it apart and replaced the worn parts and fixed all the leaks so we could send a bulldozer that was in good condition. Then I decided that there should be more than just a bulldozer. I had three more pieces of road equipment and I also bought a jeep to take along. In January 1954, with a lot of help from church members, relatives, and friends, we moved all the equipment to Richey, Montana, loaded it on the train and shipped it to the loading port in New Orleans, Louisiana. From there it was sent on to Paraguay.

"We left Montana the latter part of March 1954. Violet's parent drove us to South Dakota where we first visited. Then Harry Harder came and took us to Mountain Lake, Minnesota. From there we took a train to Chicago, then to Philadelphia, Pennsylvania, and on to the MCC headquarters in Akron where we spent a few days in orientation. Finally, on April 8, 1954, we boarded the plane with our three children, Tom, age 10, Nina, 7, and Kathryn, 6 weeks old. We arrived in Asunción, Paraguay, the next day.

"Our first impression when we arrived in Asuncion was that compared to what we were used to, Paraguay was a primitive country with its ox-driven carts, donkeys, and bare-footed soldiers. Three days later we flew on a two-engine plane to Filadelfia. This would be our home for a little more than two years. In a short time we were given a house to live in and soon felt at home. To our surprise we found fruit trees in our yard, something we had never had before.

"While waiting for the machinery we acquainted ourselves with our neighbors and the climate. Violet learned very quickly that the grocery store did not have everything needed to cook with, and soon learned how to make do with what was available. At first it was very frustrating to find out that the flour was rationed and wormy. It needed to be sifted to get rid of the worms and then warmed in the oven until it was certain that the eggs were dead. At first it was hard to eat the bread, but when I looked around it dawned on me that everyone else was using the same flour and all looked healthy. I decided to eat it and not think about it anymore.

"It took at least two months for the equipment to arrive at the river docks in Asunción. Before we could unload, our ship was shuttled to the middle of the river to make room for a ship carrying a war cannon being returned by the Argentinian government. The cannon had been taken by Argentina in a previous war with Paraguay. Stroessner had just taken over the government of Paraguay. In an effort to establish a good political alliance, Argentina's president, Peron, returned the cannon. The return of the cannon was cause for celebration in Paraguay and there was great fanfare and ceremony in unloading the cannon and returning to the government center. After two frustrating weeks we were finally allowed back to the dock to unload. We unloaded on to a river barge and two-and-a-half days later we floated into Puerto Casado. From there it traveled by narrow gauge railway to End Station, and then another 115 kilometers by dirt road to Filadelfia. The first project was to do a basement for a new creamery and next a runway for the airport. It was one and half miles long so that now DC-3 planes could land in Filadelfia.

"Now we prepared ourselves to go to work on the road project to End Station. We got all the machinery ready and built a bunkhouse to sleep in while working out in the bush. Our crew, Gerhard Brandt, Hans Teichgräf, and I, worked with the red TD18 bulldozer. Jacob Dyck from Menno Colony, his son, and Hein Frischbutter from Neuland Colony operated the yellow D7 caterpillar. Because Menno Colony had cleared the bush we could begin with the building right away. We built a road three jeeps wide [99] with deep ditches on either side, called borrow pits. We were at the roadwork about two months when five Pax men joined us – Jake Funk, Ed Ratzlaff, Carl Hooley, Phil Roth, and Bruce Boshart.

"During this time we got a new MCC director since Frank Wiens's term had expired. He was replaced by C. L. Graber. Graber had a strong interest in getting a Trans-Chaco road built and made great efforts in getting President Stroessner and his cabinet, the US Point IV, and the American and German ambassadors interested. I received a letter from Graber saying that he was going to bring these government leaders to Filadelfia. This involved two DC-3 planes that could land only in Filadelfia. A rancher, Bob Eaton, volunteered to fly them with his four-seater plane out to the job site, which was a thirty-mile flight one way. But it was unsafe to land, so he dropped a note telling me to get back to Filadelfia right away for a meeting. While waiting at the hospital they were served a luncheon. When I arrived at Filadelfia they were all there to greet me and took me inside to meet Mr. Stroessner. He shook my hand, put his left hand on my shoulder and said: 'Buller, by the road you are building with that little bit of equipment you are demonstrating to us what can be done. We will get lots of equipment and we will build the Trans-Chaco highway.'

"I was asked to head up the Trans-Chaco highway project but circumstances did not allow me to accept. I approached Harry Harder of Mountain Lake, Minnesota, who accepted and completed this arduous task. Although I wasn't able to head up this project, I was involved in some of the initial planning and surveying of the road. I was also given the task of procuring World War II surplus road equipment from the United States. Our term in Paraguay was up in June 1956 and upon our return to the US

I traveled to Washington, D.C., to locate the needed equipment and parts. Five years later we were driving on the Trans-Chaco highway from Asunción to Filadelfia.

"Another important project I was involved in while in the Chaco was helping the colonies install a generator for electricity. The generator was purchased from Germany with monies collected from General Conference churches. It was shipped to Filadelfia in much the same manner as the road equipment. However, to move the 18-ton boiler, 10-ton steam engine, and three 50-foot sections of smoke stack from End Station to Filadelfia involved building a four-wheel trailer using parts scrounged from old army trucks. The well water in the colonies was too salty to use in the boiler and water from collecting ponds was often too muddy, so a cistern was built. It was 15 feet deep, 80 feet wide, 120 feet long, and lined with brick. Gravel for making cement was unavailable so I improvised by crushing bricks baked very hard. Raising the 150-foot smokestack with the available equipment seemed like an impossible task. It was accomplished, however, by using a bulldozer and carefully placed wires and supports. It became a much-anticipated event and most of the colony's population came out to watch. Although the generator was replaced long ago, the cistern and smokestack are still in use today.

I also want to tell of our experience when I was asked to clear out the brush and trees on the north boundary of the Fernheim Colony, which was in Moro Indian territory. There had been previous attacks by the Moros on the colonies. The first attack was on the Stahl family where the father and two daughters lost their lives. The second attack was on a Menno Colony village but no casualties, only a bad scare. A third attack was in Village No. 2 in Fernheim Colony where one man was stabbed in the stomach and was left with a broken arm. These attacks caused a lot of concern and uneasiness among the people. Oberschulze Dürksen called a meeting with C. L. Graber, Robert Unruh, the Schulze of Filadelfia and the pastors of the three Mennonite churches to discuss the problems and come up with a solution to calm the people's fears. After the meeting Dürksen called me to his office and told me the plan they had decided on. The plan was to take the bulldozer I had brought, four Pax men, and two colony men to the north boundary of Fernheim Colony and cut a path about 60 feet wide. This involved clearing it of trees and brush, and building a road that could be used for traveling with jeeps. This also meant removing all tree stumps and roots.

"The purpose of the project was that, if the Moros would cross the road and come to the village, the colony people would try to surround them and capture one so they could bring him into the colony, befriend him and learn the language. I asked for a couple of days to think this over and talk to the other men and tell them of the plan. The men agreed with the plan and I told the Oberschulze we were in agreement to go unarmed and clear the brush. We went without any guns or knives, only one axe for the cook and three machetes for cutting the underbrush so we could find the boundary.

"So we went into the bush without weapons. We worked out there for two and a half months and never saw a Moro. But we knew they were around because I would find footprints all around the jeep when I left it to see how the men were doing. There were also fingerprints all over and on the bulldozer whenever we came back after being gone over Sunday. The Indians even got hold of the grease gun and made quite a mess with it.

"The five men who agreed to work on this project were capable of doing work without me, but because I had agreed to head up the project I went to visit them every day to see to their welfare and needs. The men didn't feel any fear, but the colony people were very concerned because they had no weapons to protect themselves. We know that in reality we could have been in danger, but we had put faith in the knowledge that God was watching over us, and we would be in His will should we not come out of this event alive.

"We want the colony people to know how much we appreciated their kindness, providing a house to live in and letting our children go to school. We appreciated the churches and soon learned the German well enough that we could enjoy the songs and sermons. We especially enjoyed walking to church on a Sunday morning and hearing the choir singing from a long way off. Although forty years have passed, our life in Paraguay is still fresh in our minds and we will never forget it."

12

President Stroessner Visits the Chaco Mennonite Colonies (November 12, 1954)

The editor of the *Mennoblatt*, Nikolaus Siemens, wrote the following report about the occasion: [35]

"The following six government ministers accompanied President Stroessner: General Hermojeno Morínigo (War), Dr. Fabio de Silva (Agriculture), Dr. Carlos R. Velilla (Finance), Dr. Gonzalez Milto (Education) Colonel Barrientos (Trade and Industry), Enrique Zacarias Arca (Health), as well as numerous generals, the ambassadors of the US and Mexico, and representatives from Brazil, Chile, and Bolivia.

"November 12 was a very special day for the Mennonite colonies in the Chaco and would be remembered by many for a long time to come. The visit of the president had been discussed at great length and all of the preparations had been made. The plan was to have a small exhibit in connection with this visit in which all three colonies would participate. Finally everything was prepared and in order. A few days earlier the MCC Director from Asunción, Mr. Graber, and the representatives of the Mennonite colonies – Neuland, Menno, and Fernheim – had arrived.

"Early in the morning the village residents streamed to Filadelfia. One could have asked with Schiller, "Who counts the masses, who names the names of the invited who are gathering here?" It was estimated that there were about three thousand people in the crowd.

"Around two o'clock in the afternoon the sound of a humming motor was first heard. Two twin-engine airplanes appeared on the horizon. These brought many officers from Mariscal Estigarribia (the military fort in the Chaco). A short time later several smaller fighter planes landed and finally

---

[35] In *Mennonitische Geschichtsblätter* (1955), pp. 44–46.

a larger plane appeared, painted in the colors of Paraguay and accompanied by several smaller planes. The airport was cordoned off. Only a delegation of colony representatives was allowed to be present, standing in a line to greet the important guest. Off at a distance were the high school students in blue and white uniforms, and at the gate there was a mounted guard of 18 men. Above the specially erected gate, draped with flags and decorated in green, there was a placard with the greeting, "Bienvenido Señor Presidente de la República!" (Welcome Mr. President of the Republic).

"After the propellers had come to a stop President Stroessner and his adjutant disembarked from the plane and greeted the delegation with a hardy handshake. He was followed by the Minister of War and his colleagues and generals. The students sang the national anthem and nine-year-old Elenore Thielmann handed the guest of honor a bouquet of flowers, for which he took her in his arms and hugged her.

"Twenty horse-drawn wagons and nine jeeps and vehicles transported the guests. President Stroessner and his Minister of War rode in front in a horse-drawn carriage driven by H. Neufeld of Friedensfeld, pulled two magnificent brown horses. Following them was a horse carriage drawn by two proud white horses driven by K. Ens from Schönbrunn. Riders escorted the carriages. They drove down the street, which was lined with students from the grade school. Everywhere small red, white, and blue flags were waving their greetings. At the gate of the high school grounds was a plaque reading 'Long Live the Protector of the National Economy.'

"The guests were taken to see beautifully decorated horses and a group of well-groomed black and white steers and cows. Next they were shown the attractively decorated rooms in the high school, where there were many charts, tables, graphs and other exhibits that displayed data on agriculture, rainfall, etc.

"In another room, the guests admired the handmade crafts and drawings of the students, displayed under the watchful eye of Miss Bräul.

"In the yard several small seeders made in one of Fernheim's small foundries were on display. A small pavilion made out of bricks and roof tiles had been erected by Neuland Colony to provide a demonstration of this important industry.

"The baked goods and sweet pastries produced by K. Neufeld's bakery were acknowledged with admiration.

"The guests were taken to the colony headquarters where they were led on to a stage. The crowd of about a thousand people on the other side of the street greeted the distinguished guests. Several groups of students marched past the stage, followed by an agricultural parade. First come the original oxen teams with plows, planters and cultivators. These were followed by the teams of horses representing the next stage of development, pulling plows and cultivators, disks and harrows. In the rear came the tractors, threshers and combines, etc., representing the most recent, motorized stage of development. The transport wagons drawn teams by strong horses and each loaded with 1,500–2,000 kilograms of goods were especially impressive and drew looks of admiration.

"Now came the speech welcoming the president and his retinue, delivered by the representative from Fernheim Colony, Mr. K. Walde, on behalf of the three colonies. He noted that the beginnings were very difficult because of the extreme conditions in the Chaco. Marketing of goods was also a challenge due to poor road conditions. But we were thankful for the flexibility the government had shown with respect to our religious freedom and we hoped to enjoy this freedom in the future. We were no longer immigrants but citizens of the Chaco.

"The president thanked the speaker with an embrace and designated the Minister of Agriculture to respond to the speech. He praised the extraordinary achievements of the settlers, which he attributed to their willingness to work hard and their faith in Christ.

"Finally the president spoke. As a Chaco patriot he had observed with great interest the development of the Chaco colonies and was amazed at their rapid development, even under great adversity. 'My government wants to do everything possible to assist the colonies. I promise, **indeed I assure you**, that the road from Asunción will be built. The road building equipment is already in Buenos Aires. I would like to embrace everyone in love.' Especially striking was the statement, **'Under my administration the Lopez Palace will be wide open to every Mennonite as will the doors of each individual ministry. We all are servants of the people.'** (The words about road construction were met with hearty applause from the crowd.)

"After the speeches, there was a tour of different businesses and the hospital. The guests were served refreshments in a small, shady park at Dr. Käthlers. The nurses and a group of girls from the high school offered sandwiches, baked goods and ice cold drinks, which were very welcome in the heat of the day.

"A small string orchestra played, the nurses sang several songs, and Dr. Dollinger did his best imitation of Tyrolean yodeling to entertain the guests.

"As a memento of the visit, Dürksen, the colony leader, presented a tray and walking stick made of different Chaco woods to the president, which he accepted with thanks.

"In the meantime the sun reminded one of the time. The president rose and he and his retinue went to the waiting vehicles. At the airport the guests said farewell to the large crowd. The engines started and the plane took off for Asunción, disappearing with the setting sun at 6:15 p.m."

The visit of the president was a complete success. The Mennonites had spared no effort to display their achievements. The president was clearly very impressed. This was shown by the fact that he sent reporters to the Chaco at government expense to get a more thorough report on the Mennonites. The promise to build the Trans-Chaco highway was not to be an empty promise. It was also in his interests even though it took more than two years before the work began. Nor was it clear where this highway should be built. There was as yet no plan. [36]

---

[36] Reports in the national press: "Gran Recibimiento Tribútose en Filadelfia al Gral. Stroessner," La Tribuna (November 14, 1954); "En el Próximo Año se Iniciarán los Trabajos de Construcción del Camino Orihuela-Concepción (Rio Paraguay) – Prometió a los Colonos de Filadelfia," El Pais (November 16, 1954).

13

A Study of the Chaco [37]

According to a letter from Frank Wiens in Asunción to William T. Snyder in Akron, Pennsylvania, it was James O. Babcock, Director of the United States Operation Mission to Paraguay (USOM/P), who urged Gustav Storm, the Paraguayan minister responsible for road construction, to send several American experts into the Chaco to conduct a study that would promote the Trans-Chaco highway project. It was an example of how good relationships and common interests could contribute to the development of a good cause. It is noteworthy that the essential conclusions and basic outline of this study were copied almost word for word from Fretz's memorandum of 1951 concerning the Mennonites (see chapter 6). This is yet more evidence of the close cooperation and trust that existed between MCC and the American embassy in Paraguay. Cooperation would intensify in the years to come. MCC was interested in helping the Mennonites in the Chaco and the US government was interested in the development of the Chaco. The Trans-Chaco highway project was a coming together of similar interests with different motivations.

In the forward to this Chaco study, Babcock wrote, "Paraguay today is one of the least developed countries in the world and is the most isolated and least known country in all of South America." Babcock went on to write that his study presented facts and not stories ("fiction"), facts that would contribute to the development of the latent energy and the economic potential of the Paraguayan Chaco. It should be made clear to the government that the unpopulated Chaco had great development potential as a site for cattle breeding, wood processing, agriculture and colonization.

The Chaco study contained separately paginated reports by different authors; without the maps, it was 127 pages long. It was divided into five parts and contained numerous appendices and a bibliography.

---

[37] William E. Bradford, *The Paraguayan Chaco* (Asunción: United States Operation Mission, 1955). Foreword by James O. Babcock, Director, USOM/P.

The first part deals with the history and geography of the Chaco. "Interestingly enough, in spite of its 400-year history, very little is known even in Paraguay about the Chaco, despite the fact that the Chaco comprises 61% of the national territory." Towards the end of the 19th century a small part of the Chaco was inhabited by wild Indian tribes. The Paraguayan government began to sell the Chaco by the legua (one legua equals 1,875 hectares). Until 1920 there were only a few cattle in the Chaco. The Mennonites came in 1927 and were the first to successfully colonize this desolate part of Paraguay. Readers of the report will note the author's conclusion that the Mennonite settlements are in the most fertile part of the central Chaco. It was the diverse and successful agricultural achievements of the Mennonites that led the visitors to this conclusion. In Paraguay it had been the widespread consensus that the Chaco was suitable only for raising cattle, not for agriculture.

The second part of the study described the population of the Chaco. According to the census of 1950, the Chaco had 54,277 inhabitants – not including Indians – and Paraguay had a total population of 1,406,000 inhabitants. The number of Mennonites in the Chaco was 8,005. According to department, Presidente Hayes had 23,490 inhabitants, Boqueron 28,082 and Olimpio 2,705. The most important centers of population were Villa Hayes, Puerto Casado, Mariscal Estigarribia, and the Mennonite colonies. Further colonization of the Chaco, like that of the Mennonites, was not to be expected because the necessary infrastructure was lacking; above all there was no network of roads to bring the products to market.

Agriculture in the Chaco was carried out almost exclusively by the Mennonites. The soil was very suitable for this purpose. The production of fruit was also exceptional. The problem, again, was bringing the products to market. The solution? Build the necessary roads!

Wood processing (quebracho and palo santo) on an industrial scale was concentrated at four river port towns: Pinasco, Gauraní, Sastre, and Casado. The only sugar factory in the Chaco was in Villa Hayes. "A study of the industry of the Chaco would not be complete without mentioning the special role played the Mennonites in agricultural production." There follows an impressive list and description of the economic activities of the Mennonites in the Chaco (see chapter 6, A Memorandum). The report closes with the conclusion that the Mennonites would be able to increase production considerably if there were an adequate transportation network to bring these goods to the market.

The third segment is omitted because it contains no additional information that is relevant to this work.

The fourth part provides an overview of the transportation and communication system in the Chaco. The biggest obstacle to the development of the Chaco was the lack of such an infrastructure. As well, no reliable data was available about the status of roads in the Chaco. A military map showed roads with a total length of 12,591 kilometers. In many cases these were trails left over from the Chaco War and were no longer usable, except perhaps by ox cart. There was one road from Puerto Casado that went through Mariscal Estigarribia to Villa Montes in Bolivia. This road was irrelevant for the development of the Chaco. The only reasonably good roads were around the Mennonite colonies and in the vicinity of the river ports. The study came to the conclusion that the colonization and development of the Chaco would be impossible as long as there was no reliable network of roads or connection to markets.

In December 1954 the government began building a road from Chaco-í to General Bruguez, running parallel to the Pilcomayo River. This road was without significance for the development of the Mennonite settlements. Moreover, the government planned to build a road from Concepción to Orihuela (northeast of Pozo Colorado), but even if this road were built, it too would not be a solution for the Mennonites. The study of the USOM/P concluded that there had been a lot of discussion about a Trans-Chaco highway leading through the area of the colonies but there were at the moment no concrete plans for such a project. For a few years longer, the building of a Trans-Chaco highway appeared to be a utopia dream.

Part five: concluding remarks. "Among the chief obstacles to progress in the Chaco is Paraguay itself.... Paraguay is under-developed in every respect; its educational system is weak as is its industrial base." Indeed, there were many enormous difficulties to overcome before the Chaco could be developed: distance from Asunción, the lack of export opportunities, and a hostile climate.

In spite of obstacles, however, the development of the Chaco had made great strides for several years, which was promising for the future. The

8,000 Mennonites were a 'show-case' of the kind of progress that was possible in the Chaco. They had come as destitute refugees to a wilderness that seemed to provide the white settlers with no resources for survival. "The Mennonite Colonists have successfully demonstrated through toil and faith, by blending religious and personal freedom with mutual aid, that life in the Chaco is possible." Moreover, they had proven that the necessary food could be produced in abundance in the Chaco.

Supplement nine of the Chaco study is a memorandum by a certain Mr. T. S. Darrow. He notes:

"I am convinced that what the Mennonites have accomplished in the Chaco can also be duplicated in other parts of the Chaco. Furthermore, I believe it is by far the best and richest area for agriculture and cattle ranching in Paraguay. By far the most urgent need for the Chaco, aside from the economic and political situation, is an elevated road from Asunción or Villa Hayes to Filadelfia and continuing on to the Bolivian border."

The goal and purpose of the study are unmistakable: the development of the Chaco and aid to the Mennonites in the form of a Trans-Chaco highway. To this end the attempt was made to persuade the Paraguayan government and Washington that a Trans-Chaco highway project should be a high priority and to motivate them to undertake it. This study clearly prepared the way for negotiations, among both, the Paraguayan government as well as the American embassy in Paraguay and the US government. Many people were at work to make this dream, this seemingly utopian vision, a reality.

The repeated observation that the Mennonites occupied the most productive region in the Chaco or even in Paraguay probably sounds strange to readers who know the Chaco and Paraguay. This is, however, a more common and widespread view than is realized. Years ago I was asked by an agronomy student at a national university how it could be explained that in every area where Mennonites had settled throughout their history, they seemed always to find the most productive land. It appeared they had a magic ability to sniff out the best land (the same question was asked by someone else on another occasion). I replied that his statement was not true and I asked where he had heard it. He mentioned his professor, an expert agronomist, who had told his students this in class. So I explained to him that what mattered wasn't so much the kind of land that one had but what one did with that land. The Chaco Mennonites had surely not settled on the best land in Paraguay, but they had made the best of it. This is how the claims mentioned above should be understood.

14

The Efforts Of MCC for a Trans-Chaco Highway

The Dream of a "Mennonite State" in Paraguay

MCC felt responsible for the Mennonites in Paraguay. The settlement of the Mennonite refugees from Russia in Paraguay had been made possible thanks to MCC. The German government had drawn up plans for the Russian refugees of 1930 to be taken to Brazil, but at the suggestion of MCC the larger group (a few more than 2,000 persons) went instead to Paraguay between 1930 and 1932. MCC thought that the Paraguayan Chaco would be more suitable for the Mennonites than Brazil. In August 1930, Harold S. Bender had written as follows:

> "Finally, Paraguay has one major advantage, namely its unrivalled capacity to accept the Mennonites. In January 1930, we had to accept the possibility that there would be even more emigrants from Russia and we had to find a place that could accept as many as 10,000. The Paraguayan Chaco could easily hold all of the Mennonites in the world. One large parcel of land of one and a half million hectares, totally uninhabited, was available to us. Brazil had only a limited capacity to receive this many people. So, an intelligent emigration and settlement plan required that we choose a destination where it could also be continued. We imagined a future Mennonite state where, if possible, all Russian Mennonites could re-establish and further develop their life and culture without restrictions. One additional special advantage of the Paraguayan Chaco from the cultural point of view is the fact that there is presently no culture there. There is no danger, in other words, that the Mennonites with their German culture would disappear into a foreign culture. The Mennonite community can continue to exist in Paraguay with its own faith and culture, without danger, and under the most favorable circumstances imaginable. [38]

---

[38] D. Christian Neff, ed., *Mennonitische Welt-Hilfs-Konferenz vom 31. August bis 3. September in Danzig (Mennonite Conference on Global Aid, August 31 to September 3, 1930, in Danzig)* (Karlsuhe: Verlag Heinrich Schneider, 1930), pp. 121–122.

Viewing the situation from this perspective, MCC was strongly interested, as already noted, in assisting the Mennonites in Paraguay to become a flourishing community, the longed-for Mennonite state. They spared no expense; they had accepted responsibility and they intended to do their duty. Above all, however, they were concerned to help their fellow believers in a time of need. After years of failed attempts the MCC leadership came to the conviction that the economic future of the Mennonites in Paraguay could be secured only with a Trans-Chaco highway. From then on this project would have top priority. If this could not be accomplished in the near future then the future of the Mennonites in the Chaco would be in serious doubt. Once this conviction had taken hold, what had once been only a dream would no longer be abandoned. "Nothing is as strong as an idea whose time has come," wrote J. W. Fretz in 1960, when the highway was almost finished. [39]

An Idea Takes Concrete Shape

In fact, the time for dreaming was over, it was time to make decisions. The Trans-Chaco highway project needed to be set in motion.

At the end of 1953 MCC put out feelers to LeTourneau in Peru. LeToruneau was an American, an evangelical Christian, and a major contractor. At the time he owned the largest road-building equipment in the world but, according to the MCC correspondence, was interested only in large projects. He built roads in the Peruvian jungle in order to promote development in that country. Many Mennonite Pax men were among those working with his huge machines. After some initial interest from both sides, MCC decided not to pursue cooperation with LeTourneau but did not abandon the Trans-Chaco highway project.

The MCC leadership now turned its attention to Washington and the FOA (Foreign Operations Administration), attempting to win their support for this project. In a letter of January 5, 1954, to Frank J. Wiens, MCC Director in Asunción, William T. Snyder, MCC Director for North America, wrote that the Paraguayan government needed to take responsibility for the Trans-Chaco highway project. It was too big for MCC. It would take the combined effort of many to carry out a project of this magnitude. It must be made clear to the Paraguayan government that this was not a road only from the colonies to Asunción; the road would continue

---

[39] "The Trans-Chaco Road," *Christian Living* (February 1960), p. 4.

on to Bolivia and eventually to Matto Grosso, Brazil. The road would not only promote the development of the Chaco, it would also help free Paraguay from its strong economic dependence on Argentina. Frank Wiens was given the task of gaining the support of the Minister of Public Works and Communications (Obras Públicas y Comunicaciones) for this project and seeing to the necessary studies. He was told to give the Trans-Chaco highway project high priority attention. At the same time MCC undertook to gain support from Washington, by providing qualified engineers to do the surveying and to supervise the operation and maintenance of the road-building machinery. For its part MCC was prepared to supply the personnel to operate the machines in the form of 10–15 Pax men. Young men from the Mennonite settlements could also be put to work.

When these proposals were presented to the Paraguayan Minister of Public Works and Communication, he adopted them enthusiastically and declared that he was willing to study this project together with the FOA, MCC, and the Mennonites in the Chaco. Washington too showed great openness and interest: "Interest is running high," in Snyder's words. At the same time Snyder emphasized – something he would repeat often – that the road through the Chaco must always be seen in the broader national context. Ultimately, it was the Paraguayan government that had to take responsibility for the project.

Frank Wiens asked the Mennonite Oberschulzen of the colonies for comprehensive statistical data on production, exports, and imports for the years 1951, 1952, and 1953. This data would make clear how urgent the Trans-Chaco highway project was.

On March 9, 1954, W. T. Snyder informed Dr. Willfried Mauck of the FOA in Washington that Vern Buller's road-building machines for the Mennonites in the Chaco had arrived in New Orleans and would be shipped within several weeks. Snyder also informed Wiens in Asunción that Washington was expecting a request for aid directly from the Paraguayan government. Washington urged that the initiative come from the Paraguayan government.

Concrete Steps in Paraguay

In Asunción Wiens committed himself completely to the assignment MCC in Akron had given him. His detailed letters, one on May 17, 1954, to

James Babcock, director of USOM and a second, on April 2, 1954, to William T. Snyder, Akron, give complete information about his efforts. First of all Wiens contacted Gustav Storm, the minister responsible for road construction, and laid out the difficult situation of the Mennonites in the Chaco. At the same time he also showed him the impressive economic data from the years 1951 to 1953.

The trial air service with LATN was very helpful for people who needed to travel but was not economically feasible for transporting goods. There had been negotiations for some time with PLUNA of Uruguay, but the Paraguayan government did not seem to be interested. Discussions were now aimed at getting the Paraguayan military to make a trial flight to Filadelfia with a DC-3 "this week Friday," according to Wiens' letter to Babcock. But regularly scheduled air service was not the solution needed. The Mennonites needed a direct road to Asunción. Many were beginning to leave the Chaco and emigrating, which was very alarming. Everything humanly possible needed to be done to build a highway.

Wiens made a number of concrete suggestions in his discussions with MCC Akron:

- Send "our machines to the colonies" for the Trans-Chaco highway.
- That MCC supply 10–15 men ("Pax men" – "first class operators") to operate the road-building machines.

To give the American embassy better information on the Mennonites, Wiens sent Babcock a copy of the newly published study on the Mennonites in Paraguay that dealt with historical, sociological, and economic issues (J. Winfield Fretz, Pilgrims in Paraguay, 1953).

On April 2, 1954, Wiens reported that a Trans-Chaco committee had been established:

1. Gustav Storm, Minister of Transportation, chairman
2. General Mario T. Casio, Commander of the Corps of Engineers
3. Enrique Maas, representative of the meat industry
4. Antilioso Spinzi, representing the cattle ranchers of the southern Chaco region.
5. Frank Wiens, Mennonite representative.

Minister Storm was excited about the Trans-Chaco project, but didn't deny that because of national considerations, the roads to Encarnación, Foz de Iguazú and Pedro Juan Caballero were a priority for the government. Mr. Babcock of the Foreign Operation Administration/Paraguay (FOA/P), demonstrated his active interest in the Trans-Chaco highway project by sending several experts to the Chaco to conduct a thorough study (see chapter 12, A Study of the Chaco). Wiens and Babcock agreed on the following two points:

- The Paraguayan government needed to be encouraged (interest in the project was there) to include the Trans-Chaco highway in its plans.

- A committee should be established to do a cost analysis and prepare a preliminary budget.

Wiens and Babcock were excited by how their efforts were progressing. A road from Villa Hayes through Filadelfia and Mariscal Estigarribia to the Bolivian border had been accepted as one of the projects of the Paraguayan government road-building program. Minister Storm thanked the Mennonites for their concrete offer to work together. He took the opportunity to ask if the Mennonites would be willing to help with road construction in East Paraguay. The Paraguayan government simply did not have enough personnel to operate the machines, the minister emphasized.

On April 5, 1954, William T. Snyder in Akron informed W. Mauck in Washington, that forty tons of road-building machines had been shipped to the Mennonites in the Chaco (bulldozer, tractor, self-loader, grader, jeep. See chapter 9).

In the MCC archives there is a hand-written note, which says that the Minister of War, General Juan B. Ayala, had already made a plan in 1937 for a road from Asuncion to Camacho (Mariscal Estigarribia).

Efforts at the Highest Level

At the end of April 1954, W. T. Snyder visited Washington to talk with high-level officials involved with Paraguay. He heard that there might be money available from the World Bank for the construction of the Trans-Chaco highway. In Washington they were of the opinion that Paraguay was too heavily economically dependent on Argentina and that the relationship was too one-sided. The Trans-Chaco highway would help free Paraguay from this dependence. In Washington Snyder also had a meeting with Dr. Sanchez Quell, the Paraguayan ambassador to the United Nations. From Quell, Snyder learned that the new Paraguayan president, Engineer Tomas Romero Pereira, supported the building of the highway and was very favorable towards the Mennonites. He was the one who supplied Harry Harder with a ripper in 1952 to successfully complete the road from Rosario to Friesland. On June 1, 1954, following these successful meetings Snyder, on behalf of MCC, for the first time made the following offer to the Paraguay government:

1. Eight to ten young men who know how to operate machinery and have practical experience in Peru with machines will be made available in January 1955.
2. Vern Buller, after the end of his two-year stint in the Mennonite colonies, will be involved in building of the Trans-Chaco highway.
3. All of the machinery already in the Chaco will be made available for the building of the highway. In other words, the Mennonites will supply the machines and the Paraguayan government will undertake the cost of maintaining them.

This offer was evidence of the MCC's sincere efforts on behalf of the Trans-Chaco highway. The government was willing to actively support this initiative. They were also willing to purchase any additional machines that might be necessary to build the road.

"Paciencia" – Patience is Necessary

In spite of this apparent progress, William T. Snyder, in a letter of September 9, 1954, complained about how slowly things were progressing. There had been a change of government in Paraguay. On August 15, 1954, General Alfredo Stroessner became President. Gustav Storm, a man trusted among the Mennonites, was unfortunately no longer Minister of Transportation, he was now the mayor of Asuncion. But he assured the Mennonites that he would do all he could to further support the Trans-Chaco highway project and also assured them that the new president would fully support the project. Snyder came to the conclusion that the work would have to be delayed until 1956. In another blow, it turned out that the new American ambassador in Asuncion could not be persuaded to support the project, which led to tension with the representatives of the FOA, especially with Mr. Babcock, one of the main supporters of the project.

New Hopes

Meanwhile several events awakened new hope for the Trans-Chaco highway project. [126] At the beginning of November the government began construction of a road from Puerto Elsa (Chaco-í) along the Pilcomayo River to General Bruguez. Should the Mennonites consider this route? Would this project perhaps be the first stage of a road to the colonies? An answer was not long in coming, and it was negative. Graber was of the opinion that the road to the colonies had be a direct road; in any case, there were too few machines working on this road; much of the work was being done with shovels and hoes by hundreds of soldiers. Bringing in the Mennonite young men (the "Pax boys") would be out of place here.

On November 12, 1954, as described above (chapter 12), President Alfredo Stroessner visited the Mennonites in the Chaco. This visit to Filadelfia, with a large retinue, left many Mennonites in a pitch of excitement; it was not something they would soon forget. The Paraguayan press reported this visit in detail. They also described in detail the accomplishment of the Mennonites in the middle of the remote Chaco.

On October 11, 1954, C. L. Graber reported to Akron that there was a new US ambassador in Asunción. Unlike his predecessor, the new ambassador supported the Trans-Chaco highway project without reservation. Together with Mr. Babcock from the FOA, he had already visited the Chaco and Graber was organizing a more in-depth visit. This visit was initially planned for November 8, but did not take place until November 22. Four planes flew the guests to the Chaco: a plane from the United States Air Force, a DC-3 from the Paraguayan military, and two Cessna 170s (one belonging to Robert Eaton, a cattle rancher in the Chaco, who from the very beginning had fully supported the project). Besides the numerous Paraguayan ministers, the American, German and English ambassadors, a number of engineers, technicians and other experts also participated in the fact-finding trip. In the Chaco colonies the guests were greeted by 19 different representatives from all three colonies.

An important part of visit was an excursion to see the road being built by Vern Buller, who was making amazing progress. C. L. Graber wanted these high-ranking and influential national and international dignitaries see this successful undertaking. "This is part of our efforts to get the right people interested ... so that when road projects come up for consideration a fair share is given to the Chaco." A first-hand look at the road being built by Vern Buller would serve this end, "... to impress people with what MCC had done and was capable of doing" (November 5, 1954). In other words, this visit was a deliberate preparation for the Trans-Chaco highway project. The daily newspaper *El País* [40] described with amazement and admiration how the Mennonites had transformed an Indian trail into an 80-kilometer-long road, the only link the Mennonites had with the outside world. According to the American and Paraguayan experts who took part in this visit, "There are great opportunities for the economic future of Paraguay in the Paraguayan Chaco, which comprises 61% of the national territory." The newspapers also highlighted the selfless contributions of Vern Buller as exemplary for all. *La Tribuna* (28 October, 1954) predicted that the visit would be "the inspiration ... to finding an immediate and effective solution to the various challenges raised by the lack of roads." In the *Mennoblatt* the visit was described as follows:

"On November 22 two large planes brought a large group of North American visitors from Asunción to Filadelfia. Fifteen women were among the guests; they were especially interested in the hospital and also in the school for the four deaf and dumb students in the care Mrs. Dollinger.

"While coffee was being served at the hospital, the colony leaders and the doctors as well as MCC Director Graber were present. There was a lively discussion about road building in the Chaco. Since the president's visit with his ministers there was growing acknowledgement that a road link between the hinterland and the capital was urgently needed. Every day there were headlines and reports in the newspapers, pointing out how valuable the Mennonite colonies were economically for the whole country." [41]

It is quite surprising that the activities of these high officials were given so little attention. The activities of the women, on the other hand, which would seem to be fairly peripheral, attracted much more attention.

---

[40] *"Funcionarios Paraguayos y Norteamericanos Visitan el Chaco a fin de Oberver las Obras Camineras"* (November 22, 1954).
[41] *"Besuch von 'Punkt Vier',"* Mennoblatt (December 1954).

Graber wrote to Snyder (November 27, 1954) that with this visit, the "educational phase" of the Trans-Chaco highway project was completed. Now it was time to implement the "active phase." After a look at the inventory list of road-building machines in Paraguay, Graber was convinced that brand new machines must be obtained for the Chaco, and not just one or two. But where to get these machines, if Paraguay, despite its best intentions, did not have the resources? A way must be found.

The energetic Graber already had a strategy mapped out, which he shared with his director in Akron (on November 27, 1954). The plan went approximately like this: General Samaniego, the minister responsible for road construction, had already promised two million guaraní in 1955 for a highway in the Chaco. The Finance Minister, Velilla, was also the attorney for Fernheim Colony. This meant that one could discuss these matters with him. There were plans for an audience with President Stroessner. According to Graber, the future of the Trans-Chaco highway lay in the hands of these three. With his characteristic great enthusiasm, idealism, and hard work, Graber began actively to make plans and organize. It was his opinion that the preconditions for the project were now in place.

- A Mennonite road-building committee was formed consisting of representatives from the three colonies, Abram Hiebert (Menno), Kornelius Walde (Fernheim), Waldemar Epp (Neuland), and the MCC representatives in Asunción, Bob Snyder (not to be confused with W. T. Snyder) and C. L. Graber. From now on, proposals to the government would be in the name of the Paraguayan Mennonites and not MCC.
- Point IV has already promised to provide an engineer who would work with Vern Buller on the Trans-Chaco highway. It is the explicit wish of Minister Samaniego that Vern Buller have the main responsibility for the project.
- Mr. Babcock, who had put a great deal of effort into this project as well, [130] had already sent a Dodge power wagon to the Chaco colonies.
- Robert Eaton, a cattle rancher in the Chaco, who was very keen on the project, was firmly convinced that the ranchers in the Chaco would themselves contribute significant sums of money towards building the road. He would take responsibility for this (see chapter 16).

- President Stroessner had already proposed to the American organization that the Trans-Chaco highway become a section of the Pan American highway.

Graber was hopeful that the pieces will all fall into place. If Vern Buller took on the leadership of the project and the government supported the project then things should start happening. Graber compared the work being done on the Bruguez road, where one kilometer was built in one month with a large contingent of the military, and the work of Vern Buller who, in 18 days, built nine kilometers of road and two bridges.

In Akron W. T. Snyder supported Graber's efforts and, to prove to the Paraguayan government that MCC was sincere, he suggested on November 29, 1954, that five Pax men be sent to Paraguay immediately. At the same time, Snyder emphasized to Graber that the Trans-Chaco highway was and should remain a government project, unlike the road building in the Chaco colonies, so that the government would later feel responsible for maintaining the road.

"But with Destiny's Powers …"

Things in Paraguay did not go as hoped for. There were endless negotiations that need not be described here; reading the archival correspondence is confusing and tiring. Proposals, plans and projects were brought forward and discarded in turn, once, twice, three times. Commissions were appointed, restructured, renamed, and re-established. Dates for when work was to begin were set and then postponed because the machines had not arrived, until it was discovered that they had not even been ordered yet because of the lack of funds – this in spite of numerous government promises.

For nearly two years these wearing and discouraging negotiations continued. Already in a letter of December 7, 1954, Graber was lamenting to William T. Snyder: "Bill, you have given me a very difficult assignment, to complete this road project." Snyder responded on January 13, 1955, "It is one of the most difficult assignments we have ever given anyone, but if we do not find a solution the future of the Chaco settlements is in doubt." The settlement experiment in the Chaco could not be allowed to fail under any circumstances.

In fact, the situation in the Chaco was not very encouraging. There was an unusually severe drought and many people were ready to give up. Cattle were dying because of the lack of water and pasture. People did not have enough clothing. There was little bread on the table and even less money in the bank. Graber reported that the settlers were confronting him "over and over with despairing questions." "Why had the Mennonite Central Committee even bought us to this place?" "Why has God allowed this to happen?" [42] These questions were provoked by a lack of trust in the good intentions of MCC; they were spread openly by a few. The good international reputation that MCC had gained in Russia for their relief programs during the famine (in the 1920s and later) and in Europe after the Second World War, was now in jeopardy in Paraguay. It was no wonder that under these circumstances and with opinions like this being shared openly, many settlers preferred to emigrate to their relatives in Canada or Germany. The road to distant countries was open but there seemed to be no prospect that the road to Asunción would be built any time soon. No one seemed to care that the emigration of these discouraged settlers threatened the existence of the settlements even more. Why should they care? Everyone creates his own fate….

There were some who did think about these things and feared for the future of the settlements. Over and over the words rang in Graber's ear, "If we don't find a solution …" He had looked for a solution and was sure he had found one, but not everyone thought as he did. Even in the midst of this desperate situation, where nothing was more important than unity, there were differences of opinion and disagreements, even among the Mennonites themselves. Graber often found that his well-intentioned efforts were misunderstood, but he never once considered giving up. There was no alternative but to persevere. On February 28, 1955, he wrote to Snyder: "Let me tell you in confidence that I have a very difficult role to play here. To bring the FOA, the American embassy, the cattle ranchers and the Mennonite colonies to the same point of view with respect to this road project has been and remains a terribly difficult job."

It is usually in the most critical situation, however, that the human spirit reveals itself and its capabilities. Graber didn't give up; he persevered. He wanted to help his fellow believers. Nor was he alone in this concern, although he often felt that he was. Misunderstandings were overcome and

---

[42] Christian L. Graber, *The Coming of the Moros* (Scottdale, Pennsylvania: Herald Press, 1964), p. 6

efforts continued. Over and over again it would happen that fellow believers who were convinced, as he was, that God had sent the Mennonites to the Chaco for a reason, would express their confidence in him. Life must be lived by faith in God. God makes no mistakes. Graber was convinced of this and this guided his daily work. [43]

In the US in the meantime, W. T. Snyder kept up the official contacts with Washington. Washington's position would be decisive for the future of the Trans-Chaco highway project. On March 25, 1955, he reported on a conference in Washington with officials from the FOA; the aim had been to convince the relevant people there how necessary a Trans-Chaco highway was. It was fortunate that Mr. James Babcock was also able to come from Asunción to attend the conference. In recent months the Mennonites in the Chaco had been attacked a number of times by the Moros (Ayoreos). There had been a number of victims. Babcock brought along one of the spears used in these attacks. This demonstration had a dramatic effect on the officials from the FOA, illustrating the dangerous situation of the settlers in the Chaco. Snyder reported to Graber that it had been very effective. However, despite Washington's willingness to support the Trans-Chaco highway project it was still uncertain whether the Paraguayan government truly meant business. Washington was waiting for concrete evidence that this would be forthcoming. There were also some reports concluding that it would be senseless to build a road through the uninhabited Chaco.

The Trans-Chaco Highway Project Takes Form: The Work Begins

Here, in summary, are the key events that led finally to the beginning of the project (details of the many long, drawn-out negotiations will not be repeated here):

Decree No. 6292, of February 28, 1955, made official the establishment of the Comisión pro Comino Filadelfia–Villa Hayes (Commission for the Filadelfia–Villa Hayes Highway). Graber thought, prematurely as it turned out, that Vern Buller would complete the road from Hoffnungsfeld to Loma Plata and Filadelfia by June 1, 1955. As soon as he had done so, he could immediately begin work on the Trans-Chaco highway. And if Bu-

---

[43] Ibid., p. 6.

ller took on the work using the same methods used previously, the Trans-Chaco highway could be completed in two and a half years, that is, it would be ready on December 31, 1957. As so often in this project, this proved to be a miscalculation. Later it was discovered that roads in the lower Chaco region had to be built using different methods which were more complicated and more expensive.

On May 18, 1955, the Road Construction Project Agreement between USOM/ P and MOPC was signed.

On June 18, 1955, the Demonstration and Training Project Agreement (no. 26-31-012) between USOM/P (i.e., ICA) and MOPC was signed. According to the terms of this document, the Paraguayan government was promised a first installment of financial aid in the amount of US $100,000 (one US dollar equaled 60 guaraní). The responsibilities of each partner in this project were clearly laid out. The goal of the project agreement was to train Paraguayans in the building and maintenance of roads.

=On July 13, 1955, the members of the commission for the construction of the Trans-Chaco highway were named. The members included representatives from MOPC, FOA, the cattle ranchers of the Chaco and the Mennonites.

On August 3, 1955, an event took place that greatly influenced the construction of the Trans-Chaco highway. With Decree 13.965, Paraguayan President Alfredo Stroessner officially establishes the highway commission, which had been appointed already on July 13, 1955, and also authorizes the immediate start of construction (see chapter 16).

In November 1955, Graber informed W. T. Snyder that, based on his consultations with James O. Babcock, it was clear that the beginning of work on the Trans-Chaco highway [136] had been postponed indefinitely. The reasons were these:

- The land had not yet been surveyed.
- The US $100,000 promised by Washington was not enough. At least US $200,000 was needed.
- The road-building machinery had not yet been ordered due to a lack of money and conflicting interests.
- A ferry service across the Paraguay River had to be put in place first.

14. The Efforts of MCC for a Trans-Chaco Highway

On June 3, 1956, the agreement between Paraguay and US to build the Trans-Chaco highway was signed.

On September 1, 1956, an agreement between ICA and MCC was signed. MCC would take responsibility for overseeing the construction of the Trans-Chaco highway. With this agreement Washington transferred to MCC the obligation to build the highway to which it had committed itself in the agreement with Paraguay on June 3, 1956. But this agreement was not signed by ICA until February 25, 1957. This agreement was renewed several times in the years that followed.

In October/November 1956, work began on the road between the Botanical Garden and Piquete Cué on the Paraguay River (24 kilometers).

In February 1957, construction of the Trans-Chaco highway finally began at Villa Hayes.

15

Gustav Storm

Under Presidents Federico Chaves and Romero Perreira (1953/54) Gustav Storm (born in Prussia) was Minister of Public Works and Communications. His parents had come from Prussia to Paraguay as immigrants. Storm was married to a Paraguayan but was still fluent in German. He was noted as being knowledgeable about road construction. He had brought some of this knowledge with him from Prussia (according to a letter from Graber to Snyder, March 2, 1955). He advocated strongly in favor of road construction in Paraguay.

When Alfredo Stroessner came to power on August 15, 1954, Storm became mayor of Asunción and sometime later the president of the Paraguayan Central Bank. Although he was no longer directly responsible for road construction in Paraguay, indirectly he continued to support it; since he first made contact with the Mennonites, he had also consistently supported the Trans-Chaco highway project.

In May 1955, Gustav Storm became Ambassador Extraordinary and Plenipotentiary of Paraguay to the US, with full power to take decisions. His principal assignment was to seek credits to build a water supply for Asunción and the construction of a radar-equipped airport. Storm succeeded beyond expectations and in a very short time received credits for these projects totaling 7,000,000 guaraní, a very large sum for that time. When President Stroessner heard of this, he wrote to Storm that he should immediately explore the possibility of credits for the construction of the Trans-Chaco highway. Stroessner also urged him to make contact with MCC in connection with this project because the participation of the Mennonites in this project would be most helpful.

This is how it came about that W. T. Snyder was invited to Washington to attend a meeting with Gustav Storm on May 19, 1955. At the time, Snyder had no idea what the meeting would be about.

At this meeting, which was also attended by officials from the FOA, Storm explained that both he and President Stroessner were convinced that the participation of the Mennonites in the project to build the Trans-Chaco highway was indispensable. Paraguay did not have the necessary trained personnel to operate the heavy road-building machinery. Storm went on to say that he was certain that the Export-Import Bank and the International Bank for Reconstruction and Development would make available at least US $750,000 towards the purchase of road-building machinery, if he could assure the officials of these institutions that the Mennonites would commit to working together with the FOA.[44] Sturm was now asking MCC for written confirmation that MCC would agree to oversee the construction of the Trans-Chaco highway. He would take this signed confirmation with him to the banks in order to secure the necessary credit. He was sure he would be successful.

Storm also thought that the time was ripe to begin construction of the Trans-Chaco highway as soon as possible. He himself would do anything humanly possible to make this happen. Negotiations to secure the credits to purchase the road-building machinery should take no more than three or four months at the most. Personnel to operate the machinery would be provided by the Mennonites. They would agree to train Paraguayans who could continue the work and then be employed in other road-building projects also.

Storm estimated at that time that it could take up to twelve more months to tie up all of the necessary formalities. That seemed like a long time to MCC. It turned out to be 18 months.

After these meetings, Storm, on his own initiative, visited the MCC offices in Akron, Pennsylvania, as well as the Mennonites and their schools in the surrounding areas. He told the story how he had come to know and appreciate the Mennonites during the Chaco War, and had learned that they were completely trustworthy. On this visit (on May 23, 1955), MCC gave him a copy of the book Pilgrims in Paraguay by J. W. Fretz. Snyder ended his report on Storm's visit by noting that it was his impression that Storm had felt comfortable among the Mennonites, even though MCC (and Snyder underscores this point) showed him the same hospitality they showed very other visitor (Snyder to Graber, May 24, 1955).

The visit of Gustav Storm to MCC and his readiness to advocate for the construction of a Trans-Chaco highway encouraged MCC to take concrete steps that would lead to the construction of the highway. The top priority now was to motivate the Mennonites in Paraguay to engage in the project despite their severe economic situation, a situation that appeared to be almost hopeless.

---

[44] "... provided he is assured that the Mennonites would help with personnel and management in cooperation with FOA."

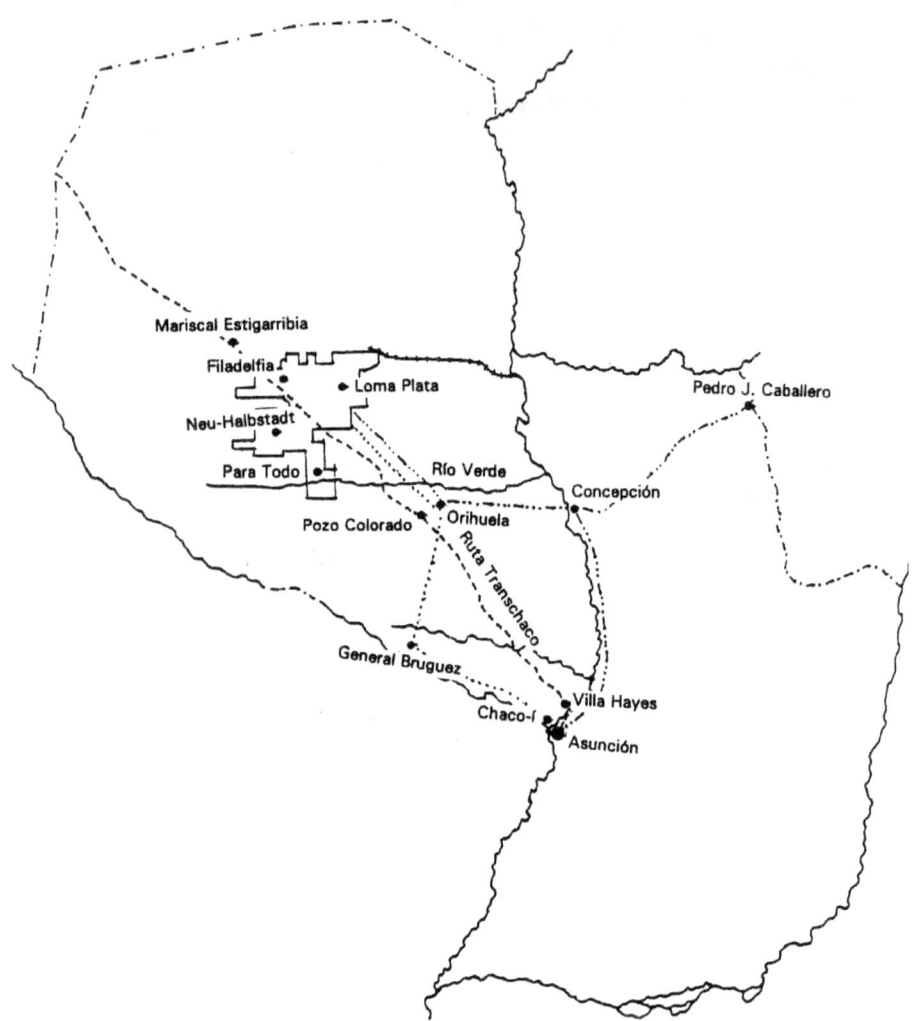

Three alternative routes for building a highway between Asunción and the Mennonite colonies:

1. Chaco-í – General Bruguez – Orihuela – the colonies
2. From Asunción to Concepción by river, then from Concepción through Orihuela to the colonies
3. Villa Hayes – Pozo Colorado – the colonies. The route that was in fact chosen.

16

Decree No. 13.965, August 3, 1955

Decree No. 13.965 provided the necessary authorization for the construction of the Trans-Chaco highway to begin. It also confirmed the Trans-Chaco commission appointed to oversee the construction, consisting of representatives from USOM/P, Point IV, the Asociación Rural del Paraguay (the Chaco cattle ranchers) and the Mennonites, and declared that the highway was a project in the national interest and with international consequences. The most important elements of the decree are summarized below.

The road-building commission was authorized to establish its own organization, to develop its own operating procedures and to make plans. It was given responsibility for oversight of the construction of the highway. According to the article 4, the construction of the Trans-Chaco highway would be financed and carried out by a coalition of four partners: the state of Paraguay, the US (Point IV), the Mennonites, and the cattle ranchers of the Chaco.

- The government of Paraguay would provide the machinery and spare parts that were necessary for the construction of the highway, and would finance the construction.
- The cattle ranchers and other landowners of the Chaco would contribute five million guaraní, more if necessary, for the purchase of diesel fuel and gasoline for the machines.
- The Mennonites would be responsible for administering the project and would supply the needed technicians and mechanics. They would bear all of the costs associated with these personnel.
- Additional unanticipated costs would be borne by the government of Paraguay. They would be added to the annual budget.

Article 5: The commission was promised complete autonomy as to how it spent its money and allocated the machinery.

Article 6: All projects, and all plans, as well as the budget had to be submitted to the Ministry of Road Building for auditing and approval.

Article 7: All of the road-building machinery and complementary materials would remain the property of the government of Paraguay. They could not be used on any other project until the highway was completed to the border with Bolivia. After the work was complete, this machinery would remain in the Chaco to be used to maintain the highway.

The contribution of the US via USOM/P, namely, Point IV, was not precisely specified in the decree. There had been talk of a Demonstration and Training Project (see chapter 18), a study of the soils in the Chaco, as well as a survey of the Chaco in order to lay out the route for the highway. This work was completed by an American engineer and paid for by the American government. Final responsibility for the technical aspects of the highway project was given to this engineer. The US government was very helpful in the task of securing credits for the purchase of the road-building machinery although in the end it turned out that most of the machinery was a gift of the US government. These machines had been built for the Korean War but had never been sent to Korea.

The Paraguayan government had three primary reasons for issuing the decree:

- Building the highway would promote cattle ranching and agriculture in the Paraguayan Chaco.
- The Trans-Chaco would link Paraguay with Bolivia and become an important artery for trade between the two countries.
- The Trans-Chaco highway would be recognized as a branch of the Pan American Highway.

The reader may have noticed that none of these reasons mention the Mennonite colonies in the Chaco. A confidential memo from the American embassy in Asunción made it clear that Article 7 was the result of a disagreement between the government of Paraguay on the one hand and the cattle ranchers and Mennonites on the other. The government insisted that the highway had to be built as far as the Bolivian border. This did not interest the cattle ranchers at all, nor was it a high priority for the Mennonites. The Mennonites, for their part, were very concerned to ensure that the road-building machinery not be used for any purpose other than for the Trans-Chaco highway. They wanted to be sure that once the highway had been built, it would be maintained in good order. Article 7 was a compromise among these various positions.

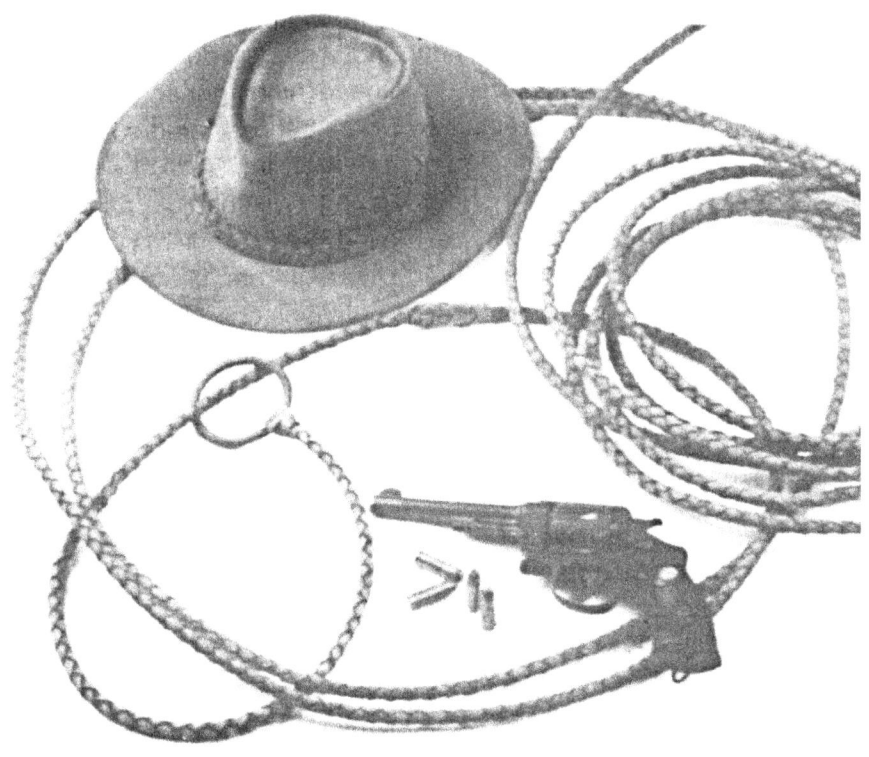

photo of cowboy hat, revolver, and cattle rope

17

Robert Eaton and the Chaco Cattle Ranchers

The cattle ranchers in the Chaco were very much in favor of a Trans-Chaco highway; in fact, they longed for such a road. They were convinced that the highway would bring them enormous benefits. One man especially had taken a strong personal interest in the project, Robert Eaton. He had been born in the US, on December 26, 1908, and had lived in Paraguay since 1929. For 11 years he had worked in Puerto Pinasco for International Products Corporation (IPC). Over time he had bought 110,000 hectares of land in the Chaco, in the region of Salazar, for US $2,000 per legua (one legua = 1873 hectares). He had been the head of the Asociación de Ganaderos del Chaco (Association of Cattle Ranchers of the Chaco) almost from the beginning of the organization. He had close relations with the Mennonites on the one hand, as well as with officials of Point IV on the other. He followed the negotiations for the construction of the Trans-Chaco highway very closely and was always ready to help or to give advice. He made his private airplane available for fact-finding flights. In 1959, when he was elected to lead the association of cattle ranchers, he sent a long and detailed memo to the ranchers (October 1956), in which he informed them where things stood and of the plans for the construction of the highway. He stressed to the ranchers their collective responsibility to raise as quickly as possible five million guaraní for the construction of the highway. Below are several excerpts from this memo. [45]

"Construction of a Trans-Chaco highway has been discussed on and off for more than six years, without there being any visible progress. The first concrete step was taken on November 22, 1954, when the minister responsible for road construction, the American ambassador, and a number of high officials visited the Mennonites in the Chaco. [He himself had been part of the delegation.] Construction of roads in and around the Mennonite colonies had started at that time, using donated machinery from North

---

[45] Robert Eaton, *"Mensaje a los Ganaderos del Chaco" (October 1956)*.

America and voluntary workers. The Mennonites claim that it is possible to build good roads in the Chaco at a relatively low cost. On this occasion, the minister responsible for road construction promised that the government would build a highway from Villa Hayes to Filadelfia.

Shortly thereafter, the President of Paraguay also visited Filadelfia and he too promised the Mennonites that a highway to the Paraguay River would be built. [Note: the visit of the President took place on November 12, not after November 22, as Eaton mistakenly has it.] On July 13, 1955, an agreement was signed by the Ministry of Road Building, the Mennonite Central Committee (MCC), the cattle ranchers of central and south Chaco, and USOM (United States Overseas Mission)."

Eaton describes the obligations of each of the four parties in considerable detail – there is no need to repeat them here.

"The cattle ranchers agreed to contribute not less than five million guaraní towards the construction of the highway. The agreement was officially acknowledged in Decree No. 13965, signed by the President of Paraguay on August 3, 1955.

"USOM/P has concluded an agreement with the minister responsible for road construction and the Mennonites to support a demonstration and training project in connection with the Trans-Chaco highway. In doing so, USOM/P has given a clear sign of its full support for the project. According to the agreement, the government of the United States of America has committed itself to contributing US $100,000, later raising the sum to US $200,000, for the purpose of buying machinery for the project. The USA is also prepared to make available two American technicians.

"The Mennonite Central Committee has committed to providing seven instructors at a cost of US $25,000. The Ministry has promised approximately US $125,000 per year for two years. In addition, 4.5 million guaraní will be allocated to the project in the 1956 budget of the government of Paraguay. On top of this, a further 1.5 million guaraní will be made available to be used to extend the highway further west, from Concepción to Orihuela. Construction of this road will be carried out by the Ministry of Defense. The President of the Republic has made it clear, however, that the stretch from Villa Hayes to Filadelfia has priority. The machines to be used for the construction of that part of the highway are currently being used on the stretch from Limpio to Piquete-Cué. The road from Avenida Artigas near the Botanical Gardens as far as Piquete-Cué is the trial run for the Trans-Chaco highway. [There follows a list of the machines already available for construction.]

"As soon as this stretch is finished, these machines as well as those that are still on their way from the US will be brought to Villa Hayes. The government of Paraguay has bought a ferry for one million guaraní and officials are in the process of buying a motorboat to pull the ferry.

"The American government has made a gift to Paraguay in the form of road-building machines that had been built for the Korean War, worth US $450,000. Paraguay is responsible, however, for transporting and if necessary modifying these machines.

"According to the agreement these machines will be used only for the construction of the Trans-Chaco highway; after the completion of the project they will remain to be used to maintain the highway.

"At the Pan American conference in Lima, Peru, last year [this is what Eaton states in his memo], the Trans-Chaco highway was designated as a branch of the Pan-American Highway. That increases considerably the value of the Trans-Chaco highway.

"A Trans-Chaco highway will give a significant boost to trade with Bolivia. A trade agreement between Bolivia and Paraguay has already been signed. The Mennonite cooperatives in the Chaco have already imported considerable quantities of gasoline and kerosene at very good prices. A liter of gasoline from Bolivia costs 5.50 guaraní in Filadelfia. When the highway from Filadelfia to Villa Montes is finished, the volume of trade with Bolivia should increase dramatically."

Eaton also mentions the many Tajamares (watering holes) that have been dug out along the highway, which will be very valuable to the cattle ranchers as places to water their cattle.

"It will be easy to build additional roads connecting the highway to many other parts of the Chaco."

The cattle ranchers needed to understand, Eaton stressed, "that the construction of the Trans-Chaco highway will involve the collective efforts of many partners. None of the partners would be able to build the highway on their own. This project would promote more collective projects. The Ministry of Road Construction as well as Point IV [149] have made the Trans-Chaco highway their highest priority. The American ambassador has given his personal support to the project. All of the cattle ranchers have a duty, therefore, to do their utmost to fulfill their obligations with respect to the Trans-Chaco highway project.

"The Comisión de Estancieros del Camino Transchaco (the Commission of Cattle Ranchers for the Trans-Chaco highway) is active and comprises the following individuals:

Chair:	*Robert Eaton*
Secretary:	*Dr. Otilio Ugarte Díaz*
Members:	*Luis Fernandes*
	Carlos Bradshaw
Special:	
Representatives:	*Atilio Spinzi*
	Adolfo Brusquetti
	Antenor Soloaga
	Federico Robinson

"*The Finance Committee is made up of the following:*

South Chaco:	Dr. Franzisco Miranda
	Dr. Otilio Ugarte Díaz
Central Chaco:	Enrique Maas
	Fernando Pfannl"

On a rainy Saturday, May 24, 1997, I sat in Robert Eaton's office in Asunción. Eaton was still an energetic, approachable, and friendly man. Despite his 89 years, he went to his office almost every day. I showed him some photographs that Harry Harder and some of his former Pax men had sent, showing them at work on the Trans-Chaco highway. That brought back old memories for him.

"Yes," he said, "I supported the Mennonites from day one in their efforts on behalf of a Trans-Chaco highway. If it hadn't been for the Mennonites, I ask myself, would the highway have been built already? The Americans were not really interested in a Trans-Chaco highway. Why should we help build a road through an area where there are no people, was their attitude.

I flew over the Chaco once with several Americans during a dry season. They reported that the Chaco was a desert. Then others came and wanted to see the Chaco, this time during the rainy season. Half of the Chaco was under water. These people reported that the Chaco was a giant swamp. Building a Trans-Chaco highway was out of the question. They called the first report a giant lie. The Americans were constantly getting in each other's hair.

"The person who was most committed to the highway at the beginning was Mr. Graber, of MCC. He was always doing something to make it happen. Today a visit to the American embassy, tomorrow at the Ministry. One can only marvel at his ability to make things happen. He organized the big visit [Eaton is referring to the presidential visit of November 22, 1954] to the Chaco. After Graber, there was Frank Wiens, and he too was fully engaged. [Frank J. Wiens had been in Paraguay already before Graber and initiated the first steps towards the Trans-Chaco highway project.] President Stroessner also supported the construction of a highway. For him the construction of the highway was absolutely necessary [this according to Eaton's understanding of the president]. He feared the Bolivians and so he wanted to settle the Chaco. [Eaton added with a grin:] He was a blood relative of the Mennonites, after all ... you know that he was of German stock? Yes, Stroessner supported the construction of the highway. The military was put to work. Machinery that had initially been intended for other projects, for example, a highway from Concepción into the Chaco, was now designated for the Trans-Chaco highway. The Mennonites insisted that for them only one route made sense, one that went directly from Asunción to the colonies.

"Work on the project began near the Botanical Gardens. It was really quite pitiful: only a few small machines. With those, you're never going to build a Trans-Chaco highway, I said at the time. At best, you may be able to build 100 kilometers of road. [He reiterated that at the time Paraguay had neither the machinery required nor the trained personnel to build a road of this magnitude.] Completely impossible. Paraguay was too poor. But later more and larger machines were brought in. One of the machines was a vehicle with a mechanical arm for loading and unloading bombs. The arm was removed and thrown into a ditch," said Eaton with a laugh.

In answer to my question, how the Mennonites had conducted themselves in the work, Mr. Eaton first explained that the young Mennonite men had done this work in place of military service. Then Eaton added that they had done very good work, both in the building of the highway and in building relationships with Paraguayans: "They all came from the farm, after all. They knew their way around machinery. Several had gained road-building experience in Peru. They really did a remarkably good job."

As for the contribution of the cattle ranchers: here things had not gone so well, in Eaton's opinion. The commission had not functioned very well: "Our contribution of five million guaraní was the equivalent, at the time, of 500 head of cattle. I was sure we could manage that. With that money, we would buy fuel and oil for the machines here in Asunción. But then President Stroessner solved our problem in another way. He added an extra tax on fuel, and all of the revenue from this tax was directed towards the Trans-Chaco highway. Also, the government contracted with Williams Brothers to build I don't know how many kilometers of the northern part of the highway. They had made themselves available, and they had the machinery to do the job."

"Yes," said Mr. Eaton in conclusion, slowly and reflectively, "the Trans-Chaco highway changed the Chaco for good, and this process is still continuing. When the American engineers laid out the route that the new road was supposed to follow, I was there. I made sure that the highway would run close to my property. It was a huge benefit for me, but it has also brought me a great deal of trouble in the last few years."

18

The Contribution of the United States: Point IV in Paraguay [46]

US bilateral aid to Paraguay began in 1942. Three relief organizations were set up in Paraguay during the Second World War; their mission was to promote the development of Paraguay, which was, according to common opinion, the least developed country in South America. 1. A health care organization, the *Servicio Cooperativo Interamericano de Salud Pública* (SCISP), was created in May 1942 and worked in cooperation with the Ministry of Health. 2. An agricultural organization, the *Servicio Técnico Interamericano de Cooperación Agrícola* (STICA), was established in December of the same year and operated in cooperation with the Ministry of Agriculture. A series of Mennonite Pax men served in this organization; it can even be seen as a forerunner of the Trans-Chaco highway project. The goal of the organization was to improve Paraguay's agricultural production and thereby to improve the standard of living. 3. In 1945 the *Servicio Cooperativo Interamericano de Educación* (SCIDE) was created; it worked in close collaboration with the Ministry of Education.

These relief and development organizations in Paraguay were under the direction of the *Instituto de Asuntos Interamericanos* (IIAA, the Institute for Inter-American Affairs) in Washington, which was led by Nelson Rockefeller.

There were changes to the programs of the organizations after the end of the Second World War. The Marshall Plan was created to help in the development of sixteen European countries and to prevent them from falling into the orbit of communism.

President Harry S. Truman, in his inaugural speech in 1949, formulated his program for foreign aid as a weapon in the war against communism.

---

[46] *Embassy of the United States of America, Historia de la asistencia de los Estados Unidos al Paraguay, 1942-1992: Cincuenta años de cooperación para el desarrollo. Asunción, Paraguay, 1992.*

There were four points: Point 4 of his program (hence the name of the organization) would prove to be significant for Paraguay and lead to various kinds of aid. The goal of 'Point IV' was to provide technical assistance to underdeveloped but so-called free (that is, not communist) countries so that they could achieve economic prosperity. Point IV was an economic weapon, in other words, which was intentionally used by the Americans to prevent the spread of communism in countries of the Western world.

Point IV also led to a restructuring of organizations working on programs of the American government. In February 1952 Point IV was introduced to Paraguay. Until then the three American relief organizations had worked independently of each other. Each organization had its own director and reported directly to the appropriate authority in Washington. Now they would all report to the same director, namely the director of the United States Overseas Mission (USOM). The first director of USOM in Paraguay was Albion W. Patterson, who had been director of STICA since its founding. He was responsible for the coordination of all American foreign aid in Paraguay.

Patterson had already made contact with the Mennonites because of the Mennonites Pax men who served in STICA. J. W. Fretz too now contacted Patterson (see the memorandum of J. W. Fretz, August 24, 1951), to talk to him about the possibility that Point IV would support the construction of a Trans-Chaco highway. Without the support of Point IV for the Trans-Chaco highway project, the highway would not have been built when it was.

The aim of this book is in the first place to describe the contribution of Mennonites to the construction of the Trans-Chaco highway. For the sake of completeness, however, the two projects of the US government need also to be mentioned. In part these projects contributed to the construction of the Trans-Chaco highway but, more importantly, they were decisive for the economic development of the Mennonite colonies and beyond.

On October 30, 1959, the government of Paraguay signed a contract with the Williams Brothers Company to build 130 kilometers of the northern stretch of the Trans-Chaco highway, that is, from the colonies to the north. Williams Brothers was a pipeline engineering and construction firm based in Tulsa, Oklahoma, and had built several hundred kilometers of road in the northern part of the Chaco on behalf of Pure Oil Company, which was drilling for oil in the region. They had a million dollars' worth of machinery, which they were eager to use for road construction elsewhere in Paraguay; they were an obvious choice to build more roads in the northern part of the Chaco. In the southern part, it was sometimes impossible to work on the highway for months on end because of the amount of rain; hence the work progressed very slowly. Since interests coincided, the government of Paraguay and the Williams Brothers Company quickly came to an agreement. This contract was later extended to include the stretch from Mariscal Estigarribia to the Bolivian border. [47]

The other contract was not directly related to the construction of the highway, but was no less important for the economic development of the Mennonite colonies. The two factors came together; the two supported each other and their combined contribution to the development of the Chaco was greater than the sum of the parts: a road to markets, and the capital needed to increase production. This took the form of a loan of one million US dollars at very attractive rates of interest, payable in 30 years, which was arranged by MCC as intermediary and designated for the Menno, Fernheim, and Neuland colonies in the Chaco and for Volendam and Friesland in East Paraguay. The agreement for this loan was signed in Washington already on May 9, 1957, by the Paraguayan ambassador to the US, Osvaldo Chaves, and Samuel Waugh of the Export-Import Bank.

A reporter from Voice of America was present at the signing and asked the Paraguayan ambassador to say a few words over the radio to his fellow citizens. Among his words were the following:

"On behalf of the government of Paraguay I have just signed an agreement in the offices of the Export-Import Bank for a loan for the Mennonites in Paraguay.

"It is important to make clear how immensely important the impact of this agreement will be for us, for the settlements in the heart of the Chaco that are striving to move forward especially, but also for Paraguay as a whole.

"The loan of one million dollars is intended to help increase agricultural production, modernization, and to build the foundations of an industrial base that will transform raw materials into finished products."

---

[47] MCC News Service, "New Company May Help Speed Up Trans-Chaco Roadway Project," *The Canadian Mennonite* (October 23, 1959), p. 3, and "Paraguayan Government Signs Road Contract," *The Canadian Mennonite* (November 27, 1959), p. 5.

The ambassador stressed that the loan was not just for the Mennonites in the Chaco but also for Volendam and Friesland colonies in East Paraguay. He concluded:

"Through Voice of America, I am able to share the joy that it gives me to sign this agreement on behalf of our government, an agreement that will have a great impact, and I send my sincere greetings especially to the Mennonites but also to all of my fellow citizens in Paraguay. Thank you very much." [48]

Professor J. W. Fretz argued that the million-dollar credit meant as much for the economic development of the Chaco colonies as did the Trans-Chaco highway. He sees this loan as the consequence of an important article of the Mennonite faith, namely the notion of the community as a brotherhood of accountability, an accountability that transcends national boundaries. MCC made itself responsible for finding an affordable source of credit for the Mennonites and assisted them in the negotiations to obtain it. Fretz stresses that the efforts of MCC were motivated by "the enormous concern of North American Mennonites for the future of their fellow believers in Paraguay." [49]

When the Trans-Chaco highway was finally ready near the end of 1961, the Mennonites had received and invested approximately one-third of the credit (US$ 347,600). Pasture and crop lands had been expanded, many tractors, harvesters, and numerous other agricultural implements had been bought. Together with the completion of the Trans-Chaco highway, the million-dollar line of credit was the catalyst for the transformation that led to the present high standard of living enjoyed by the Mennonites in the Chaco.

---

[48] *MCC News Service, "Paraguay's Ambassador Voices Gratitude for Chaco Loan," The Canadian Mennonite (June 7, 1957), p. 3.*
[49] *Fretz, 1962, p. 155.*

19

A Demonstration and Training Project

On June 18, 1955, the minister responsible for road construction, General Marcial Samaniego, on behalf of Paraguay, and Cliffort A. Pease, Jr., representing the American government, signed an agreement to establish a Demonstration and Training Project – Construction and Maintenance. The Demonstration Project to build roads and maintain them was a generous overture on the part of the American government to help Paraguay to develop its elementary network of roads. This project was to be developed in close connection with the construction of the Trans-Chaco highway. The stretch from Jardín Botánico to Piquete Cué (24 kilometers) along the Paraguay River was chosen as the first component of the project. The contribution of USOM/P consisted of US $100,000 to be used to purchase the necessary machinery. (In July 1956 a further US $100,000 was added). In addition, two Caterpillar D7 bulldozers and two Caterpillar D8 angle dozers, two Number 12 graders and three Number 70 scrapers were purchased. USOM/P also contributed an engineer, who would oversee the technical aspect of the work.

The project had four goals:
a) To demonstrate the good roads could be built efficiently and affordably.
b) To demonstrate how inexpensive it was to build bridges and drainage culverts.
c) To train locals in the proper operation and maintenance of the road-building machinery.
d) To train locals in the proper care and maintenance of existing roads.

Mennonite Central Committee (MCC) was an important partner in this project. MCC undertook to be responsible for the following:

1. To make available as many as seven mechanics, who have experience and competence working with road-building machinery and with the construction of roads and drainage culverts.

2. The training of local workers who can then be sent to other construction sites in Paraguay
3. Responsibility for all costs for Mennonite personnel.

This then was the contribution MCC agreed to make to the project. Other partners were the cattle ranchers of the Chaco and the Paraguayan government.

The Expectations of USOM/P of This Project

USOM/P expected that a sufficient number of local workers could be trained in the operation and maintenance of the road-building machinery, and that these workers could then be employed in other areas of Paraguay where roads needed to be built: for example, the road leading directly from Asunción to the border with Brazil, the road to Pedro Juan Caballero, etc. The Paraguayan government had already developed a plan according to which all of the larger urban centers in Paraguay would be connected directly to Asunción. The road to Encarnación was almost ready at that time.

The USOM/P also hoped, moreover, that Paraguay would be able to maintain these roads in good condition; regular maintenance would be required because of the anticipated increase in traffic. If this goal could be achieved, then, USOM/P hoped, "the construction of good roads will free Paraguay from its economic stagnation and begin the process of dramatically increasing its productive capacity and opening new opportunities for trade with all three of its neighbors, not just with one."

The Reasons Motivating the Training Project

The reasons are given in detail in the "Description of Project and Reasons for US Financial Support," and are summarized here.

The Paraguayan road network, or, more precisely, the lack of a network of roads in Paraguay, is given as the most important reason. Paraguay had very few roads. Goods were transported almost exclusively by water and the 312-kilometer railway network. The network of Paraguayan roads was barely 2,000 kilometers long. A useful point of comparison: as of today (1997), the Mennonite colonies in the Chaco have, over the years, built and still maintain a network of roads totaling more than 3,000 kilometers. These were built using only the resources of the colonies. In Paraguay at the time, 65 kilometers were paved and another 200 kilometers approximately were graveled; the remaining roads were fair weather only; when it rained they were no longer useable.

The lack of good roads was one of the biggest stumbling blocks to the economic development of Paraguay. Only 4% of the country's land mass was utilized, 96% lay completely uncultivated. The few agricultural areas that existed were completely isolated and had no, or no economically viable, connection to the market. Paraguay had a lot of good, productive land, which could not be utilized to the full because of the lack of adequate roads. Paraguay could produce a lot more food than it needed and export the surplus to neighboring countries. At that time this was possible only in the case of Argentina. There were no roads connecting Paraguay to Brazil or Bolivia.

The Mennonite colonies in the Chaco can serve as concrete examples of this situation. In the 25 years since the first colony, Menno Colony, was founded, the Mennonites (8,000 settlers in three colonies) demonstrated conclusively that agricultural products could be produced in large quantities in the Chaco, an area formerly written off as marginal. The Mennonites were so successful, the USOM/P discovered, that the Paraguayan government had allowed them to negotiate a trade agreement with Bolivia. The Mennonites would be allowed to export their agricultural products to Bolivia and import the necessary fuel. A highway from Asunción to the colonies and from there on to Bolivia was, therefore, an urgent necessity. Paraguay, however, did not have the resources and in any case its priorities lay in East Paraguay and a transportation link with Brazil.

Because the Paraguayan government had already made public its support for a Trans-Chaco highway, and because both the Mennonites and the cattle ranchers had committed themselves to providing financial support (US $300,000) as well as labor for the project, USOM/P saw sufficient grounds for supporting a Demonstration and Training Project, with a value of US $100,000. Sometime later the contribution was raised to US $200,00 and eventually to US $250,000. The agreement of June 18, 1955, was revised several times, on August 29, 1955, and on June 30, 1956.

19. A Demonstration and Training Project

According to a June 27, 1955, press release of the Foreign Operation Administration (FOA), it was just as important to promote recognition of the need to maintain the network of roads in Paraguay as it was to build new roads. In 1954, for example, Paraguay built 160 kilometers of new roads. In 1955, one year later, these roads were no longer useable, because they had not been maintained. The Demonstration and Training Project, and the agreement with the government, were intended to make sure that this would not happen to the Trans-Chaco highway.

20

The Agreement between the American Government and MCC

On June 18, 1955, the American government and Paraguayan government came to agreement on the Demonstration and Training Project. On September 1, 1956, MCC was invited to take on responsibility for carrying out the agreement, and MCC committed itself to doing so. According to the terms of the seven-page agreement, MCC agreed to fulfill the following tasks and obligations:

a) To train personnel to operate road-building machinery and to build roads.
b) To train local workers in the best use of the machinery.
c) To carry out experiments to determine the most cost-effective way to build good quality dirt-based roads.
d) To demonstrate how dirt-based roads can be maintained in the best possible condition.
e) To demonstrate how to build cost-effective bridges and drainage culverts.

In order to carry out these tasks, MCC committed itself to making available up to 20 skilled technicians and mechanics. These persons had to have practical experience with operating the machines and building bridges and culverts. They would be responsible for giving the local workers chosen by the Ministerio de Obras Públicas y Comunicaciones (Ministry for Public Works and Communications) the necessary practical training.

The International Cooperation Administration (ICA) would also make available a road-building engineer, who would work closely together with the MCC workers and who would be responsible for overseeing and carrying out the project. The ICA would be responsible for his needs: wages, trip costs, room, and board. He would be the one ultimately in charge.

The ICA would finance the acquisition of all machinery and tools that were needed to carry out the project. These would remain the property of the ICA, but would be handed over to MCC without conditions until the project was complete.

MCC would be responsible for the bookkeeping and accounting, and would submit a report every six months at least, detailing the work accomplished in that time period. When the project was complete, it MCC would submit a final report on the project.

The Mennonites were forbidden to engage in any form of religious or political proselytizing while they were working on the project.

The agreement was initially for a period of two years, but was then renewed several times.

The project began at the Botanical Gardens and General Artigas Street and ran a distance of 24 kilometers to Piquete Cué on the Paraguay River. At the end of December 1956, this first stretch of the highway was finished. The Ministry of Road Building bought a ferry for one million guaraní to transport the machinery across the Paraguay River to Villa Hayes. In February 1957 it was possible to begin the construction of the Trans-Chaco highway in Villa Hayes.

Here one particular factor should be mentioned, which dramatically increased the speed at which the Trans-Chaco highway could be built. USOM/P had made available US $90,000 for the purchase of machinery for the Training Project. This was enough to buy only a few new machines. All of sudden the opportunity arose to purchase surplus road-building machinery, which had been intended for use in the Korean War. These "surplus war materials and machines," valued at US $450,000, were available for US $90,000. Some of these could already be brought to Paraguay and put into service by October 1956. The words of the prophet Isaiah seem appropriate here: "They will beat their swords into plowshares and their spears into pruning hooks" (Isaiah 2:4). Machinery that had been intended for war, was here literally transformed into road-building equipment, to serve the interests of economic development and peace.

In addition, the Paraguayan government placed an order for machinery with a value of US $25,000. It is not known whether this machinery was ever used in the building of the Trans-Chaco highway.

When it came to choosing the route of the highway, an important concern was to make the road as straight as possible, while at the same time taking advantage where possible of land of higher elevation and those areas where it would be easiest to cross the rivers.

United Nations Peace Symbol

21

Harry Harder Builds the Trans-Chaco Highway

Towards the end of 1956 work on the Trans-Chaco highway could finally begin. The responsibility had been transferred to MCC. This again was under the direction of Harry Harder who had been in Paraguay in 1952 and who had been called to carry out the work under the supervision of an American engineer. Since there are no activity reports available about the work on the road and no correspondence exists from the years 1959 to the end of 1961 we will let Harry Harder himself, after nearly 40 years, tell us about the work on the Trans-Chaco highway. (this is an abbreviated version).

"In 1956 I was again asked by MCC to go to Paraguay to be in charge of the Pax men and work on the Trans-Chaco Road. I felt it was God's will that I go for two more years.

"My family and I and six Pax men arrived in Asunción in September of 1956. We all stayed at the MCC Home for the first six months. The Pax fellows were from 18 to 25 years old.

"Only two had former experience in this kind of work. Road building started the day after we got there. My wife Anna was very concerned about the education of our children, Martin (13) and Margaret (9), since they could not speak High German or Spanish. The MCC arranged to send the Calvert Correspondence course work and Anna did the teaching.

"We first built the road from Asunción to the river port, Piquete Cue, twenty-four kilometers. When this work was done, we took all the equipment across the river on a 25-ton ferry. The trip across was about three-quarters of a mile. A building was rented for the storage of parts and supplies. The Pax men and I lived there, too, with a Paraguayan cooking for us. We all went back to Asunción for weekends. The Trans-Chaco highway began at the northwest corner of Villa Hayes. For several weeks the Pax

Harry Harder with his family (H. Harder)

men operated all the equipment in the forenoons and trained Paraguayan civilians and military people – lieutenants, sergeants, and soldiers – in the afternoons. This was a good experience for all of them.

"The road plans were to clear a 100-meter right of way through the bush and jungle. The road was to be one meter above high water level, and eight meters wide. No ditches were made. All the soil used for roadway came from borrow pits along the sides of the roadway. At times there was up to three feet of sand on top of where we made the pits. This was bulldozed to the side until good soil was found. Pits were 75 feet wide and 150 feet long and up to 25 feet deep.

"Some of the men did not like to operate bulldozers. I told them that as long as they did not learn to operate bulldozers real well they would never get a chance to operate a Tournapull scraper. It did not take long then to get real good on a dozer. We worked five days a week in two shifts – 7 am to 1 pm and 1 pm to 7 pm. The Paraguayans that were appointed to us became good machine operators.

Harry Harder with the Pax men at the Caterpillar plant in Peoria, Illinois, before their departure for Paraguay (MCC)

"We set up our next camp at Cerrito and then set camps spaced about fifty kilometers apart. From Cerrito there were a lot of jungles, swamps and water.

"One forenoon we got to a water-covered area, and we all wondered what we could do next. I sent the operators to go for their noon lunch and I stayed to figure out how to continue. I used one of our best bulldozers to push the mud and water off an area where we wanted to make a borrow pit so dirt could be hauled to where the roadway went. When the operators came back from lunch, it was ready for them to go to work. We had to do this for many kilometers.

"To make this decision was really not my responsibility, but Point IV engineers were not always present. Then I was forced to make the decision myself and act on it. This happened quite often and never caused a problem with the engineer. Point IV was agreeable to this.

"Even before my two-year term with MCC was finished, the Americans asked me if I wanted to keep working for them in the future. I agreed and kept working for Point IV till the Trans-Chaco highway was finished. Point IV had three engineers, one in the office in Asunción and two on the Trans-Chaco highway. I replaced one when I started to work for them. The Pax men and the men from the Mennonite colonies remained under my direction. I still fully supported them.

"Another time we had been following the surveyor's course and got to a bad swamp. We knew that going through there would delay us a long time, so I went to Asunción to talk to the Point IV chief engineer. That evening he happened to be celebrating his birthday with some of his friends but he took time to talk to me. I told him about the swamp and suggested going around it. He agreed, so I changed the course and went around the swamp. Soon afterwards he came to check and he approved it. At a much later date he came to me and said that if it had not been for the Mennonites, the road could not have been finished.

"About once a month I went to Filadelfia by plane. There I picked up a Point IV vehicle and drove to where the surveyors were working to check or fix equipment. We had two D8 Caterpillar bulldozers, one motor grader, one four-wheel drive truck with winch and a four-wheel drive power wagon with winch for the surveyors.

"The work on the south end of the road was much more difficult than on the northern end because there was more rain, more bush and jungle and more rivers to cross. One hundred to two hundred Paraguayan civilians and military personnel were assigned to the project and received training in road and bridge construction, machine maintenance, etc. Along with them were thirty Pax men and a dozen men from the Mennonite colonies. We also had two Paraguayan doctors.

"The military had three large barracks, one mess hall and kitchen, two buildings for officers, and one bakery. The bakery had a trough one foot deep and six feet long. They put bread dough in it and two barefoot soldiers kneaded it with their bare feet.

"In swampy areas we dozed mud and water until we got down to solid ground. In real bad swamps we used draglines. We never took out more mud than we could fill back up with good dirt the same day, because if it rained during the night the area would be filled with water.

"This worked fine until later when we got a new engineer who had di-

21. Harry Harder Builds the Trans-Chaco Highway

Eating lunch: Harry Harder and the Mennonite workers, seven Pax men and one each from Menno, Fernheim and Neuland (Harry Harder)

fferent ideas about working in mud and water. He took several of our best bulldozers and dozed out all the mud and water for a half mile. We got a heavy rain and it filled the half-mile section with water. Then he gave orders to put our big draglines in there to take out more mud. These machines sank three feet into the mud but finally they got the mud out. Later he agreed to do it the way we had done it before he came – never to take out more than could be filled in the same day.

"Progress was always delayed when we got to a river. To get across we had two thousand-gallon pontoon tanks which we put into the river and grouped together. Then we put 12" x 12" timbers on top of them to form a 12' x 30' pontoon platform. We then tied this to the riverbank where we wanted to cross over.

"The first machines to cross over were several bulldozers to clear the trees off so we had room for other machines. Next was the crawler tractor with a big winch to winch other machines on to the pontoon. Last were the Tournapulls. One time the last one to go across got a little bit to one side of the pontoon. The pontoon tilted and the Tournapull slipped into sixteen feet of water. The Pax fellows tried to fasten a heavy cable to it for several hours but could not do it because the drawbar where they wanted to fasten the cable was under mud. Finally I showed a Paraguayan how to fasten the cable on another scraper that was standing nearby. He then took off most of his clothes and went down under water with the one-inch cable. He had to come up for air once but when he went down the second time he got the cable fastened. We then fastened that to the winch tractor cable and winched the Tournapull out.

"The plan was to skip higher stretches or dry spots of road way during the dry season and build roadway in the low areas. After doing this for some time it rained hard so all the equipment was isolated because of the water between camp and the machines. What to do?

"We got the military to cut lots of palm trees into twelve-foot sections and place them side by side across the soft places. We could then drive small trucks across with supplies and fuel and operators to the equipment. In some places we had to use motorboats. After the wet section dried up we went back and finished the roadway.

"One day the mechanics had just finished overhauling a Tournapull engine which a Paraguayan lieutenant had been operating. After he started using it again it got very hot. He had forgotten to fill the radiator with water. The engine was ruined.

"Usually when careless things like this happened in the military the people involved were treated very severely. Most of the time they were given fifty stripes with a whip and their heads shaved. This time the Paraguayan captain who was in charge of all the military men on the project asked me what to do with this lieutenant. I told him ill-treating him would not do him any good. Rather I told him we needed a new man to be in charge of greasing and fuelling all the equipment and I would put him in charge of it. He would get five or six soldiers to help him. The captain agreed. The lieutenant thought this job was beneath him but he had no other choice. He turned out to be one of our best servicemen.

"On another occasion three escaped soldiers arrived at noon time and shortly thereafter a military jeep arrived looking for them. The soldiers began to run, trying to escape. They were shot at but no one was hit. A sergeant on horseback caught one with a lasso and dragged him to the camp.

Building a bridge. In the middle one of the Pax men wearing a 'Pax Service tee-shirt'
(D. K. Yoder)

"We used a four-wheel drive truck that had a large fuel tank on it, plus several barrels of different kinds of oil which were used in different machines. The men drove to where the machines were working and stopped one machine at a time to service it. It usually took about half a day to finish all the machines.

"While the road was being built, military guards were stationed every 50 kilometers. If it rained, all traffic was stopped along the new road, sometimes for several days or until the road dried off. I was lucky; I got a pass to go on the new road anytime.

"Point IV always supplied me with a four-wheel drive vehicle with a winch on it. This took me all over. Sometimes I had to travel miles in mud and water. Often the water got so deep that it ran into the pickup cab. Once I even took off the fan belt so the fan would not get the ignition system wet. But I never got stuck.

"We hauled our drinking water from Asunción for the first eighty kilometers. Later, water was hauled from the lagoons in the Chaco. Sometimes cows, horses, frogs and other animals were seen in the lagoons. Our camp doctor tested the water and said it was safe to drink.

"The military bought meat from the ranchers and the Pax men bought it from the military. The Pax men brought most of their food along from Asunción when they had been there for the weekend. If I went to Asunción during the week I would always stop in at the MCC Home to pick up mail and food for the Pax fellows.

"Fuel and gas were hauled from Asunción on a 4,000-gallon transport truck. Almost all welding and repair work was done by our personnel at the campsite. More complicated work, such as crankshaft grinding and lathe work, was taken to Asunción to one of the Mennonites, Victor Koop."

"Pax man" Leland Stalter teaching young Paraguayans how to weld (Harry Harder)

Koop reports that Harder usually brought equipment in need of repair on Friday night. On the same evening he and his workers would start the repair work. If necessary they would work all night long and sometimes even on Saturday. On Monday morning Harder could take the equipment back to work.

Harder continues:

"A young Paraguayan was in charge of all parts and supplies. He was as honest a man as can be found. We could not have wished for someone better. We tried to have parts for all of our equipment at all times. When I ordered parts from the United States, it took close to a year before they arrived. Several times I went to Brazil to the Caterpillar factory to buy parts."

To the question why spare parts were so scarce, Victor Koop said the machines that were sent to Paraguay were old models.

In many cases they were no longer being manufactured. Spare parts could not be obtained through the representative in Asunción. He also explained that the sand in the Chaco was the biggest problem for the machines. It was a very fine dust that consisted of decomposed organic sea life (it is thought that at one time the Chaco was a sea) which had accumulated over centuries and penetrated into every nook and cranny. This dust caused more damage to the machine than the sand.

Harder continued:

"Most of the machines which we were using for the Trans-Chaco highway were built for the Korean war and different environmental conditions. Most of them were many years old but had never been used. They had to be rebuilt for Paraguay conditions. Some machines were taken apart and sent to us in crates. We put them together in the Chaco.

"Our heaviest piece of equipment weighed 28 tons. We took it across the river on a 25-ton ferry. This was risky. These machines (Link Belt draglines) were used mostly to change the course of the river by making new channels and working in swampy areas, but also for pile driving for bridges. Some of them went down as deep as 40 feet. The wood for the bridges was delivered by a Mennonite in Bergthal in East Paraguay, John Janzen.

"The construction of the Trans-Chaco Highway was a very difficult undertaking for many reasons:

1. The soil in the southern part was especially unsuitable. There were many swamps, rivers, bush, jungle and insects. The climate was difficult.
2. Most of the workers came inexperienced. We had to deal with language problems, cultural differences and different life styles. In practical life this is not always easy.
3. Many machines and tools were of inferior quality and not build for the demands of the Chaco. This meant more repairs and replacement parts.

"I felt that working relations with the military were good, also with Paraguayan civilians, colony Mennonites and Pax men. Problems which arose could always be solved in a satisfactory way.

"Ferry service across the Paraguay River left much to be desired. The ferry had a capacity of 25 tons and was pulled by a smaller boat that had only a car engine in it. It made crossings every two hours during the day. After some time the car engine gave out. We then got a 200-horsepower diesel engine with a propelling unit attached to it. We mounted in on a small ship which we used for some time. Later we got a 160-ton ferry from Japan. It had two diesel engines mounted in the center with two propellers on each end of the ferry. It could load a number of trucks on it, two side by side, and the ramps were operated electrically.

"Once when it was time to move camp during the dry season, a lieutenant and I were driving along a rough and bumpy trail that a bulldozer had left. We were going through an area where a lot of trees had been dozed out the width of the dozer. It was hot and dusty.

"Soon we came to a place where a lot of people were standing on the other side of the river. We stopped and talked to them. They told us that a tree had fallen on a lady and injured her back. They had no way of getting her to a doctor and hospital and asked if we would take her. We told them we would. They brought her across the river on a boat and into the van on a cot. Many people wanted to go along but I told them only two besides the sick lady could go along.

"The trip was very painful for her because the trail was so rough and it was dusty and hot. Finally we got to the hospital but they would not take her in until they were paid for the expenses of her care. She did not have enough money so I paid for her. They were very thankful for the help we had given them.

"Another time our camp doctor and I were on the way to camp from Asunción when a Paraguayan lady flagged us down and told us that her husband had a severe cut in the groin area and was losing a lot of blood. We picked her up and went on a narrow trail through the woods to the place where he was lying on a blood-soaked cot. We loaded him into a van, with the cot, and took him to a hospital which was only six miles away. They said that we had made it in time.

"President Stroessner came to the road project quite often. Several times when we crossed the river on the ferry the president and his guards were there, too. We visited together. He was always interested in what was going on at the road project.

"One time he came by plane and landed on the road. Military men from camp went to pick him up with a jeep and they went hunting close to a Mennonite village. They got stuck in a mud hole, so one of the guards was sent to the Mennonite village to get help. Several boys came and pushed the jeep out. After they got out, the President took the Mennonite boys with muddy clothes and shoes to Asunción and gave each one a new pair of shoes and a new military uniform. They stayed in Asunción for several days and then he sent them back to the colony by plane.

"Point IV had a program to send two Paraguayan civilians to the US for training in mechanics for a year. I got the chance to pick one and chose a young man from one of the colonies. He spent six months at the Caterpillar training center in Peoria, Illinois, and for six months he was at a larger Caterpillar dealership, overhauling Caterpillar equipment. When he finished his course he had to spend a year in the Trans-Chaco repair shop. He stayed longer and I picked him to be the shop foreman. He did a lot of work on bulldozer undercarriages, tracks, rails, rollers, and sprockets. Working in sand and water is very hard on bulldozer tracks.

"I am thankful that during the construction of the Trans-Chaco highway there were no serious accidents. When you think that I had so many inexperienced people to deal with it seemed like a miracle. On Pax man, Clair Brenneman, lost two fingers. Once I was crushed between two motor graders. We radioed for the Williams Brothers plane (they were working on the north end of the road from Bolivia) to pick me up from Filadelfia and take me to the Asunción hospital. X-rays were taken but they found no broken bones.

A visit to the highway project. From left to right: Frank Wiens, MCC, Heinrich Dürksen, Oberschulze of Fernheim Colony, Jakob Reimer, Oberschulze of Menno Colony, Harry Harder, and Peter Derksen, Oberschulze of Neuland Colony (Harry Harder).

"In spite of many difficulties, the work load, and disappointments, I did enjoy the work on the Trans-Chaco highway and did it willingly. One of the biggest problems was the inexperience of the workers sent to me. Of the 30 Pax men and a dozen young men from the Mennonite colonies only two had experience when they began working. All the rest had to be trained on the job. But they learned very quickly and did good work, also in training the Paraguayans. As a rule the Pax men stayed two years; some stayed longer. They did their work in the spirit of Christian service. They invited the Paraguayan soldiers to their Bible studies.

"Point IV was in Paraguay not only for the Trans-Chaco highway. They were also involved with the road being built from Concepción to Pedro Juan Caballero. A Brazilian company did the work. My Point IV boss often took me with him to check up on that project. After the Trans-Chaco highway was finished, Point IV started another project from Colonel Oviedo going north past Friesland Colony. I worked there several months until my term was up.

"My boss wanted me to come back for another term but I said I wanted to quit. He then asked me if I would consider another term in another country. I told him it depended on where it would be. Then he told me that I should stop in at the Washington DC office on our way home. We did and I accepted a job with the Bureau of Public Roads in north-eastern Brazil. Twelve men were sent, three for the Recife office and one each for each of the nine states."

A few months after I received this report from Harry Harder we heard the news that he had died on April 26, 1997. The Trans-Chaco highway is a monument to his efforts in Paraguay.

The machines available to him for the Trans-Chaco highway:

5 4-wheel-drive pickups
14 bulldozers
6 1H Heil scrapers
6 Tournapull
5 motor graders
1 crawler winch tractor
2 motor cranes
4 drag lines
1 fuel transport (4,000-gallon capacity) with tractor
1 school bus
1 fuel-and-grease maintenance truck
1 welder service truck
1 20-ton lowboy trailer with tractor
2 five-ton flatbed trucks
4 one-and-a-half-ton flatbed trucks
2 pile-driver leads
1 sawmill with power unit
1 well-drilling machine with power unit
2 turning lathes
1 120-ton track press
1 rock crusher with power unit
3 arc welders and cutting torches
   diesel pump and injector testing equipment
   most tools for all repairing and maintenance
   pontoons for crossing rivers

The following US Pax men and voluntary service workers from Canada worked on the Trans-Chaco highway under the direction of Harry Harder:

Floyd Bauman, St. Jacobs, Ontario
Bruce Becker, Kitchener, Ontario
Elmer Bontrager, Hartville, Ohio
Clair Brenneman, Kalona, Iowa
Tony Brown, Altona, Manitoba
Virgil Claassen, Whitewater, Kansas
Bob Ediger, Topeka, Kansas
Emmanuel Erb, Berlin, Ohio
Jake Funk, Des Chenes, Manitoba
LaVerne Graber, Freeman, South Dakota
Peter Harder, Phoenix, Arizona
Richard Hershberger, North Judson, Indiana
John Huebert, Henderson, Nebraska
John Kauffman, Iowa City, Iowa
Wayne Kauffman, Archibald, Ohio
Marvin Klassen, Mountain Lake, Minnesota
Walderma Klassen, Manitoba
Herman Konrad, Clearbrook, British Columbia
John Kratz, Soudertown, Pennsylvania
Leslie Nafziger, Archibald, Ohio
Jim Plummer, Waterloo, Ontario
Bill Rupp, Wauseon, Ohio
Richard Schmidt, Goessel, Kansas
Leland Stalter, Chenoa, Illinois
Lynn Troyer, Wellman, Iowa
Delbert Wiebe, Whitewater, Kansas
Delmer Wiebe, Whitewater, Kansas
Menno Wiebe, Winnipeg, Manitoba
Daniel Keith Yoder, Kalona, Iowa
Ezra Yoder, Kalona, Iowa

Young men from the Chaco colonies who worked on the Chaco highway (accurate as far as Harder was able to remember):

Heinrich Bargen, Neuland Colony
Heinrich Boschman, Fernheim Colony
Hans Dick, Menno Colony
Rudy Eckert, Fernheim Colony
Heinrich Epp, Fernheim Colony
John Janzen, Tres Palmas (later Niverville, Manitoba)
Hans Neufeld, Menno Colony
Isaak Regier, Neuland Colony
Jacob Sawatzky, Menno Colony
Peter Thiessen, Neuland Colony

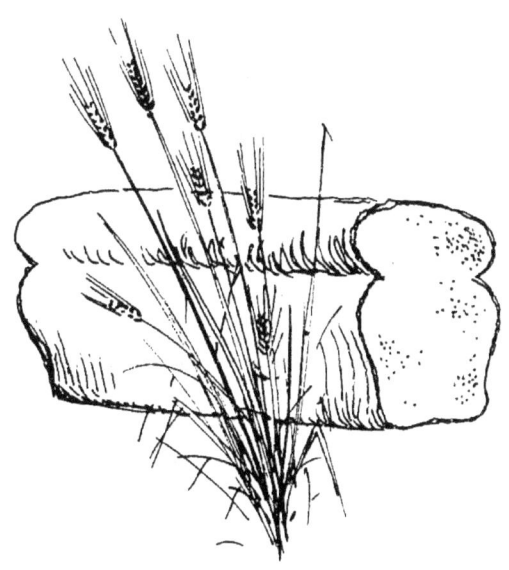

22
"The Tran-Chaco Highway Is Ready"

On October 5 a limousine drove down the main road of Filadelfia, followed by a truck full of soldiers and a military police vehicle with siren blaring. It was the President, Alfredo Stroessner, who had not wanted to miss the opportunity to be the first to travel by limousine on the newly built highway between Asunción and Filadelfia. The Mennonites had already beat him to the punch with their transport vehicles, he said in his welcome speech.

On October 4, the final stretch bridging the north and the south end of the road had been completed, a monumental day in the history of the Chaco. True, some of the bridges were not yet ready, but because of the generally dry conditions, the distance could be covered without much difficulty in several hours.

The Oberschulze of Fernheim and Menno had gone to meet the President at the spot where the road was finally completed and then accompanied him to Filadelfia. The President and his staff entourage were entertained under the shady trees, before he continued his journey by plane on to Nueva Asunción on the border with Bolivia.

While they were eating, the director of the secondary school in Filadelfia, Peter Neufeld, gave a short speech of greeting. He said: "This is a historic moment for the Mennonite colonies in the Chaco. When you, Mr President, deigned to visit the colonies in 1954, you promised in your speech to see that the Chaco would be linked by road to Asunción. Our hopes have now indeed become a reality. In the vast, isolated Chaco, work on the road was begun from both ends and met yesterday at Km 219. Two giant arms gave each other their hands, and confirmed the promise made years ago. The opening of this highway tolls the bell for a new era in our lives, with new hopes, but also with new challenges. We thank you, Mr. President, and the Paraguayan government, for your active intervention to make this work come to pass."

The President responded: "I did not make you a promise at that time, rather, I gave you assurances that this highway would be built. It was always of deep concern to my government that this project be completed. It has cost us many millions, but we are proud of it. I fought in the Chaco War and saw a lot of combat, but I have never been so moved by any experience as I am now by the enormity of this realization, that this 400-kilometer-long highway has been completed. We are convinced that because of this highway, a new era for the Chaco has begun. The Chaco is no longer isolated, and much that was formerly impossible will be possible from now on.

"But we need to keep going. The highway is to be completed as far as Mariscal Estigarribia and then to the Bolivian border, across the Parapití as far as Santa Cruz. From there it will run past Cochabamba and join the Pan American Highway.

"I have greatly longed to see this moment, and I am very happy that I am able to experience it. We will continue to assist you, and we are happy that because of this highway your economic situation will improve."

"One of the generals concluded by praising the good will of the President, and his efforts. Among other comments, he noted that "the President had this road built not because he is a politician but because he is a statesman. A politician has the next elections in mind, the statesman thinks of the good of the country."

The official dedication of the highway was to take place at a later date.

The first truck to reach Asunción via the Trans-Chaco highway, September 4, 1961 (MCC)

23

"The Servant has Done His Duty …"

In October 1961 the Trans-Chaco highway from Villa Hayes to the Chaco colonies was completed. There was widespread joy about this. The obligations undertaken by MCC and the Mennonites were not yet fulfilled, however. They were ready to keep working on the stretch of highway to Mariscal Estigarribia and, if necessary, to the Bolivian border. There were, however, certain obstacles, which made it difficult to continue the work and at times prevented it altogether. One of these obstacles was that the money promised by the government did not always arrive when it was promised, or not at all. Until now the ministry responsible for road construction (the MOPC) had been responsible for oversight of the project, but now the Ministry of Defense was insisting that it be responsible for the construction of the highway. In the midst of this tense situation, the MCC Director in Asunción received a letter that made him suspicious; it must have seemed like a pail of cold water had been poured over him. Here is the text of the letter in English translation:

Ministerio de Obras Públicas y Comunicaciones

Asunción, February 7, 1962

Señor
Director del Comité Central Menonita
Presente:

As Director of the Trans-Chaco highway, I have the privilege of contacting you in connection with the invaluable contributions of the Mennonite organizations to the major national project, the first phase of which, Villa Hayes to Filadelfia, has now been completed.

I will not attempt to express the gratitude these contributions have earned, since any words I might use would certainly be completely inadequate to express the appropriate gratitude. I would like to state for the record, however, that the Mennonite Central Committee has earned itself a prominent place in the history of Paraguay, its second Fatherland. Your descendents will look back with pride on the work you have accomplished; and you too should look with even greater pride on the fruit of your labours, which, according to the agreement, have now come to an end.

It is with great satisfaction that I can inform you that you may withdraw your personnel from the work on the Trans-Chaco highway. Please convey to each one of them my personal heartfelt thanks for their efforts that they gave, without losing heart, for the completion of this great task.

Sin otro particular, I take this opportunity to give you my warmest greetings,

Eng. Basil A. Fiddes
Director
Trans-Chaco Highway

The intent of the letter was clear: "The servant has done his duty, the servant can depart." The game, however, that is being played in this way, is puzzling. Peter Epp, to whom this letter was sent because he was in charge of the MCC office in Asunción in the absence of Frank Wiens, did not know what to make of this letter. He went to the offices of Point IV and showed it to Ted Moorehouse. Moorehouse was also taken aback; he had heard and suspected nothing. There had to be some misunderstanding. In his view, it was absolutely necessary that "the boys keep working on the Trans-Chaco highway." Moorehouse promised that he would straightaway write a letter to the Paraguayan Ministry of Defense – it was quite clear that this ministry had now taken over responsibility for the Trans-Chaco highway project – so that "the Mennonite team would stay on the job of the Trans-Chaco highway."

Peter Epp wrote a letter with these details on February 15, 1962, to MCC Akron. In this letter, Epp mentions also that the Director of Point IV, Mr. Russell, and the American ambassador to Paraguay, Mr. Snow, had suddenly and unexpectedly been recalled to Washington for consultations. It would be advisable for William T. Snyder to meet these people in Washington, in order to hear directly from them about what was happening. In the meantime, the Paraguayan government had reached an agreement with Williams Brothers, according to which this company would build the 120-kilometer stretch of highway from Mariscal Estigarribia to the Bolivian border. The agreement with Point IV to build roads in Paraguay would expire at the end of June, and the agreement with MCC at the end of March. Epp closes his letter to MCC with the following laconic and confidence-inspiring words: "Our boys will keep working on the highway till the end of March. In the meantime William T. Snyder and Frank Wiens will have the time and opportunity to discuss long-term plans with the responsible persons, whoever these might be." [198] The Mennonite men remained on the job. Perhaps the letter reflected only the hasty, unreflective personal views of Engineer Fiddes. He remained in his position, but under the authority of the Ministry of Defense.

On April 27, 1962, William T. Snyder wrote Wiens that it was very difficult to work with Fiddes, that he was "unrealistic" and "as changeable as the wind." The highway was finished as far as the Mennonite colonies and it had been in constant use since the day it had opened. It had become clear immediately that it needed regular maintenance if it was to remain serviceable. Long stretches had already become unusable, especially the final 150 kilometers to the north. More and more frequently, especially during bad weather, travellers were coming across the dreaded 'bariers' across the highway erected by the military. These 'bariers'kilomet bore the sign: "Highway closed," which was strictly enforced. Something had to be done. The ministry responsible for roads turned to MCC and the Mennonites in the Chaco, and asked them to make available the necessary personnel to maintain the 420-kilometer stretch of highway from Villa Hayes to the colonies. The government declared itself ready to pay for the machines, spare parts, fuel and oil.

At the end of March 1962, William T. Snyder came from MCC headquarters in Akron, Pennsylvania, to Paraguay, in order to see the situation for himself and to speak to the people involved. He then presented to the Ministry of Defense the guidelines for future cooperation (April 5, 1962) that had been agreed to in discussions, for the repair and maintenance of the highway.

1. In the future the Ministry of Defense would negotiate directly with the Mennonites in the Chaco and MCC would negotiate separately with the Mennonites ("by sub-agreement").

"Ruta clausurada" (Highway closed)"

2. The Ministry of Defense would be responsible for providing all of the necessary machinery, spare parts, fuel and oil. The Mennonites would provide the personnel, either from the colonies or through MCC.
3. The Ministry of Defense would supply an engineer to provide technical oversight for the work.
4. The Mennonites in the colonies would be tasked by MCC with negotiating the details of the agreement with the Ministry of Defense. MCC would give them clearance to do so within two weeks.

The agreement to maintain the Trans-Chaco highway would be completely separate from the agreement to build the highway. Snyder concluded his letter: "We hope that after the completion of the stretch of highway from Filadelfia to Mariscal Estigarribia, the Mennonite personnel will be promptly reassigned to the project to maintain the roads, and that part of the team now stationed in Montelindo can begin immediately with repairs on the Trans-Chaco highway."

These guidelines, which were strictly adhered to by William Snyder, were the foundations for future cooperation. On April 28, 1962, Frank Wiens wrote to Ted Moorehouse at the American embassy: "We have committed ourselves, that our team (a) will continue to work on the construction of the Trans-Chaco highway as far as Mariscal Estigarribia and (b) that it will take over the maintenance of the highway as far as Filadelfia, until we as MCC and the Mennonites from the colonies feel that we have fulfilled our part of the bargain." Harry Harder was asked to organize this new project and to provide the technical oversight. Final responsibility for oversight would, however, remain with the Ministry of Defense. It was not possible to determine how long the Mennonite personnel maintained the highway. In any case, the Oberschulzen of the colonies soon protested and proposed that the Mennonites be responsible only for the northern stretch of the highway.

All of the details can no longer be recovered, but on June 19, 1962, Frank J. Wiens wrote that the construction of the stretch to Mariscal Estigarribia was not going well, and the Engineer Fiddes and General Careaga, who were responsible for maintaining the highway, were of the opinion that the Mennonite personnel should be used only for the maintenance of the highway.

Oberschulze Jakob Reimer of Menno wrote to Wiens on December 3, 1962, that the military was very unhappy with the behavior of several of the Pax men, and wanted to send them home as soon as possible. The complaint was that they followed their own rules and did whatever they wanted. The military preferred the Mennonite men from the colonies. Unfortunately it could not be determined if this complaint was an isolated case, whether the complaint was checked and substantiated, and how the issue was resolved. The mood remained tense. Years later, on a visit to Paraguay, Frank Wiens explained the situation as follows: relationships with the government were actually always very good. In the final year of construction on the Trans-Chaco highway, it was sometimes our impression that the military no longer had such a favorable impression of us and that they wanted to take the responsibility for construction of the highway away from us.

However that may be, MCC now felt that it should bring its involvement with the Trans-Chaco highway to a close. On May 13, 1963, Frank Wiens informed the three Oberschulzen of the Chaco colonies that "MCC has completed its active participation [in the Trans-Chaco highway project]." Cooperation on the work to build the Trans-Chaco highway had lasted for six years, the stretch to Mariscal Estigaribia was finished, "and our contribution as Mennonites had become smaller," Wiens modestly added. He then compares this modest contribution with the "loaves and fishes" at the feeding of the five thousand. A modest contribution, but one, that brought forth a great modern miracle. Many more than five thousand people would be fed in the Chaco because of the construction of the Trans-Chaco highway. The "servant" could leave. He had completed his work faithfully and had left behind an important national project that he had helped to bring about. The Trans-Chaco highway was the beginning of a new era for the Chaco in general and for the Mennonite colonies especially. From now on, the development of the colonies would not be hindered.

24

A Devastating Judgment: Project Performance Unsatisfactory

Frederick C. Catton and Norman A. Kotz were commissioned by the USAID Mission to Paraguay to evaluate the performance of MCC on the work of building the Trans-Chaco highway. Their report, submitted on May 24, 1963, reached the devastating conclusion: "Audit Rating: Unsatisfactory."

An important part of their evaluation was to determine to what extent MCC had fulfilled the obligations it had undertaken in the agreement with the ICA (International Cooperation Administration); namely, its performance in the so-called Training Project.

In the first place, the auditors regretted that the written records necessary for their evaluation and reports were lacking. They were clearly annoyed by this. Consequently, their evaluation had to be based on oral interviews with the staff of MCC, the ministry responsible for road construction, USAID/P and some other persons. Their audit covered the period from September 1, 1956, to September 1, 1960. The auditors based themselves in the first place on the goals of the agreement and the Training Project, which were to train Paraguayans in the construction and maintenance of roads, bridges, and drainage culverts, and to operate and maintain the road-building machinery. The primary goal was to train Paraguayans so that they could take over the Paraguayan national road-building program. This Training Project was to be an integral part of the Trans-Chaco highway project. The audit lists the obligations that the Mennonites had agreed to take on (see chapter 19).

The audit report determined that, according to one memorandum and a number of oral reports, the Trans-Chaco project began with 10 Mennonite men between the ages of 17 and 23. Several had experience operating farm machinery, but most had no experience at all in operating road-building machines. Eight of these men had taken part in a two-week training course at the Caterpillar plant in the US before they came to Paraguay. Only one had been a certified technician, and two had some experience with road construction. One had a general knowledge of mechanics. Not one of the men had any skill or experience building bridges or drainage culverts.

The audit continued: In the years 1958 and 1959, the first group of workers was replaced with Mennonites, some who came from North America, others from the colonies in the Chaco. With few exceptions, all of these men had to learn on the job. Seven of the nine had had two week's experience working with LeTourneau before they came to Paraguay. According to data it provided to the auditors, MCC supplied a total of 31 men to work on the construction of the Trans-Chaco highway. There were never more than 16 at any one time. A total of 16 men were from the Mennonite colonies, but there were never more than four Paraguayan Mennonites working on the project at any one time.

A record of the personnel at issue and their qualifications could not be found in the MCC office. From conversations it was plain that many of the men coming from the US found the living conditions in the Chaco very frustrating.

The lack of documentation concerning the training that these workers had received before or during the project was the most serious obstacle preventing a proper assessment of whether the conditions of the agreement had been met.

The auditors determined that only seven Paraguayan civilians and 23 soldiers received thorough training in the operation of the road-building machines. In the end, only five soldiers were trained to become qualified mechanics.

In the Ministry of Defense, the auditors found 47 certificates printed for military personnel and civilians who had worked on the Trans-Chaco highway, which were supposed to have been handed out in 1958 in recognition of the work completed. These were never handed out because they had typographical errors. According to oral testimony, however, only 31 of the 47 had qualified to receive such a certificate.

Sixteen Paraguayans – civilians and soldiers – had had more or less adequate training before they began working on the project. It had probably been these men and not the Mennonites who had given instruction to the inexperienced Paraguayans chosen by the Ministry. No theoretical training in a classroom was ever given. Everything had to be learned by observation in the practical work itself. Naturally, the result was that many mistakes were made and some of the machines were damaged beyond repair. This had been a very expensive method of training, was the auditors' conclusion. One of the biggest obstacles to carrying out the work had been the lack of replacement parts.

The auditors found no evidence of deliberate wrong-doing.

MCC had never written regular progress reports, nor a final report, although this was required according to the agreement.

There were no personal records for the workers supplied by MCC – neither for the workers nor for the technicians.

This audit report had necessarily to be based on oral reports and interviews, which were, understandably, to some degree contradictory and of varying quality and reliability, as the auditors noted. On the basis of the information and impressions they had gathered, they came to the following conclusion: "Our assessment of all of these oral reports and the incomplete documentary record leads us to the conclusion that the conditions of the contract were carried out unsatisfactorily."

The MCC Director in Asunción Responds

It was not possible to determine whether MCC ever officially responded to the auditors' report. There is a response, however, in the form of a letter from the MCC Director in Asunción, Frank J. Wiens, which he sent to Robert Miller of MCC in Akron, Pennsylvania. This letter is most informative. Wiens acknowledges that in many of the details the auditors are correct, but on several points he suggests that it is possible to come to different conclusions. He names several:

1. The report appears to hold MCC primarily responsible for the training of local workers, without acknowledging that ICA too had some responsibility for this. Wiens points to Article 3 of the agreement, according to which ICA agreed to work closely with the civil engineers building the roads and took responsibility for overseeing

and directing the project. The auditors did not take this contractual responsibility of ICA into account. Nothing is said about it. Wiens commented: "Throughout the time of the agreement, it was always our understanding that ICA was overseeing and directing the project. They simply didn't have anyone who could do this …" He pointed out, for example, that the 47 certificates had been printed at the request of and signed by both the ICA and the ministry responsible for road construction – "but not by MCC." According to Wiens, therefore, MCC was aware of its obligations.

2. Wiens questioned, moreover, the emphasis that the auditors placed on the Training Project, without mentioning what was in fact the fundamental goal, which was to build the Trans-Chaco highway. These two goals had been inseparable, however. The primary goal of the project had always been the construction of the Trans-Chaco highway. All four of the partners in Paraguay had focused their attention almost exclusively on the construction of the highway. The possibility of a Training Project had been an afterthought, and had rarely come up in discussions even while the project was underway. This same attitude had been shared even by Point IV.

3. According to Article II.0, practical training was the goal of the agreement. Neither MCC nor ICA, Wiens contended, had ever considered that this would include regular classroom instruction with textbooks. The focus had always been on 'practical' training. This was the intention of the agreement and this is what had been implemented.

4. According to Wiens, the auditors were wrong to conclude that the training of the Paraguayans had been carried out by Paraguayans and not by Mennonites. It may be true that the Mennonites had first trained Paraguayan officers, who then passed along the knowledge and skills they had learned to other Paraguayans. But, as Wiens pointed out, this was in fact an effective training method.

5. Furthermore, in disagreement with the auditors' report, Wiens strongly emphasized that the Mennonites men had come with much better skills and training than suggested by the auditors.

6. The accusation that no reports had been written applied equally to the ICA, not just to MCC, wrote Wiens.

Wiens also emphasized that the auditors took no account of the exceptional situation in Paraguay, and had not really grasped the limitations imposed by local conditions. The term 'technician' needed to be more precisely defined in future agreements so that both partners would share the same understanding of this term.

In light of his comments, it seems that Wiens did not attach a great deal of importance to the auditors' report; he for his part found it unsatisfactory also. The Trans-Chaco highway was finished. Everyone in Paraguay was very happy about this. An unfavorable report of an auditor writing with the benefits of hindsight, would finally not change anything about the fact that the highway had successfully been built.

The auditors carried out their evaluation at precisely the same time that there was some tension between the military and the Mennonites – the only tensions we know about – and at the same time that Engineer Fiddes, Director of the Trans-Chaco highway, wanted to dismiss the Mennonites. This, in fact, probably had some influence on the auditors.

The auditors' report shows, indirectly, how much responsibility had been given to MCC and how much trust national and international organizations were willing to place in it. Perhaps the scale of the assignment was a bit too much for a relief and development organization that was founded to feed the hungry and clothe the naked "in the name of Christ." But there can be no doubt that MCC had done exemplary work.

> This book first appeared in German in 1998, followed by a Spanish edition in 1999. On both occasions, the response of readers exceeded my expectations. Those who responded to the Spanish-language edition were primarily elderly persons who had had some involvement in the building of the Trans-Chaco highway. Some came to see me in person, others contacted me by telephone. An engineer who had worked on the final stage of the highway told me, "It happened exactly like you described. Mr. Fiddes could be quite unpredictable; he caused many problems." Another person asked which chapter of the book was the most important. I put the question to him: "That's what I'd like to hear from you." He replied, "The chapter on the highway and practical theology." I asked him to elaborate. He answered warmly, "If we would act according to the principles you outlined in that chapter, Paraguay would be a very different place." All of those who contacted me agreed on two things: If the Mennonites had not been involved, the highway would never have been built; and that, on the whole, their work had been exemplary.

25

Pax Men – Experiences from the Trans-Chaco Highway

Literally translated, "Pax man" means "man of peace," "pax" being the Latin word for peace. This was a program of MCC in which young Mennonite men from the United States, during the years 1951–1973, could serve a two-year term, as conscientious objectors, in lieu of military service, on a Christian-motivated development project in a foreign country. A few young men from Canada also served under this program, even though Canada had no compulsory military service. They did this service as voluntary Christian-service workers.

Several young men from the Mennonite colonies in the Chaco also worked for two years, in some cases longer, on the Trans-Chaco highway (unfortunately there is no official list of names). The following are reminiscences from a few of these men in chronological order. The reports were written down from memory by men who were now much older and wiser. The dates in parentheses are the time they served in Paraguay.

Edwin Ratzlaff (United States 1954–1956)

"I was a member of a group of 10 men who went to South American under the direction of the Mennonite Central Committee (MCC) as an alternative to military service. This opportunity was a chance for us Pax men to live out our profession of faith and serve God and country.

"Our group initially worked in Peru before half of us were sent to the Trans-Chaco project in Paraguay. Our group included a civil engineer, Bruce Boschart, an airplane pilot, electrician and architectural and engineering mechanic, Phil Roth, a farmer, Jake Funk, and myself, who had road building experience. We arrived in Asunción on December 21, 1954.

We were met at the airport by C. L. Graber, Margaret Braun, Sara Penner and Robert Snyder, MCC workers in Asunción at the time. After a few days in Asunción we went to Filadelfia on December 30. Our main mission was to work on the Trans-Chaco highway from Asunción to the colonies. However, the machinery we needed for the Trans-Chaco project was delayed in customs so we worked on inter-colony roads and other MCC and colony projects.

"The road project was under the direction of Vern Buller who had donated a bulldozer and other road machinery to the colonies. After building a bunkhouse for us to live in at the road project site, we began work on a road from Filadelfia and Sommerfeld colonies to End Station where it connected with the railroad line to Puerto Casado. The road had previously been used but only in dry weather. We graded it up to allow the water to run off. We also made some bridges where there were drainage problems. At places we worked in open range and at other places we needed to clear brush and trees.

"We also built about 40 kilometers of road in the Filadelfia area and another 40 kilometer road to Neu Halbstadt and Neuland. On another 40-kilometer road on the Moro Clearing we had only a compass to guide us. When we reached our destination we were amazingly only three feet from the stake that was set as our terminal point.

"We worked on other projects when we were not able to work on the road project. Some built an electric line in Neu Halbstadt. I worked with Bob Unruh, breaking sod with the MCC tractor, and then at KM 81 with Dr. John Schmidt.

"Food was provided from Filadelfia. Some of the men helped with the preparation. We also did some hunting for fresh meat when we could. I remember eating small antelope, ducks and some wild edible bird meat.

"We returned to Filadelfia every other weekend and worked on the road projects the other weekend. For vacations some of the men went to Brazil, Argentina and Uruguay where there were other Mennonite settlements.

"Bob and Myrtle Unruh were the leaders of our unit of five Pax men. We had a number of North American leaders visit us who gave us encouragement. The leaders of the colony also encouraged us. We enjoyed the fellowship and singing with the church choir.

"Some of us, like myself, grew up speaking plattdeutsch (Low German) at home and High German in church. The ones who did not know German when they came could speak some after eighteen months.

"My life was much enriched by the opportunity of service as I interacted with missionaries and helped meet some of their needs. I always looked forward to the Sunday services and participating in musical events in the churches on special occasions. In fact, I was the first to furnish organ music in Filadelfia at the wedding of Annie Neufeld and Eldon Brandt of Hillsboro, Kansas, and at the funeral service of Kornelius Neufeld.

"My experience was a confirmation of my faith and the teachings of the Mennonite Church. It was a time of studying the Scriptures for myself and giving of myself in this Christian service. I learned to trust God in time of uncertainty, especially when my faith was tested during some of our trying circumstances.

"I particularly remember the time the Moro Indians attacked in Filadelfia. We were asked to make a clearing north of Filadelfia in hopes that the missionary team would be able to make contact with the Indians. They were able to do this but Missionary Isaak lost his life in the process.

"The possibility of contact with the Moro sometimes had us rather on edge. One day as I was backing the bulldozer, I noticed that my partner who was setting stakes began putting on quite a scene. He had been surprised by an Indian who was hunting in the area. He feared that the Indian might be a Moro but we were relieved to discover that he was not."

Menno Wiebe (Canada 1955–1957)

"For the first 18 months I served as an agricultural experiment worker in Volendam Colony. The second period of my involvement took place on the Trans-Chaco highway during the last six months of my assignment.

"I came from a farming family in British Colombia, which involved work with various machines. I also had truck driving and logging experience.

"I was prompted to do Christian service in Paraguay following strong appeals made by two prominent Mennonite leaders, the late Frank C. Peters and Peter J. Dyck. Dyck challenged the youth of the Mennonite Educational Institute to consider rendering service for the Lord. 'If your non-Mennonite neighbors are prepared to enter military service to defend the country, what kind of commitment are you peace-loving Christians prepared to give?' My decision followed. I was also motivated by a hunger for a global perspective on Christianity, on cultures of the world, and on needs in areas of poverty, racism and oppression.

"The job on the Trans-Chaco highway brought with it a daily routine consisting of rising early in the morning. We slept on cots in a large hall of the military base camp. In the morning we washed up in a basin of cold water situated outside the building, drying ourselves on towels hanging from the wash line. After participating in a circle of maté drinking friends, we responded to the breakfast bell, breakfast being served in a dining shack. After breakfast of coffee, galletas, and sometimes jam, we went off to work on the road-building equipment.

"My job was that of operating the large crane which was used for loading crushed rock, digging trenches and sometimes operating road-building equipment. When not occupied on the crane, I worked either with the No. 10 Heiliner earthmover, with a Tournapul earthmover, or on the 10-30 International bulldozer used for blazing the trail.

"We stopped for lunch, usually at the base camp when we were not too far removed. Lunch consisted of rice, soup, galletas and occasionally some dessert. For supper we often had bean soup, beans, rice and locally purchased meat. Almost always there was garden produce to serve as a basis for salad.

"We drank tea and coffee during the meals and supplemented our fluid intake with the always present guampa and bombilla.

"All meals were shared with the Paraguayan soldiers, an occasion to get to know them quite well. These interactions afforded an opportunity to learn both Spanish and some Guaraní. The eating together and sharing in the tereré (Paraguayan tea) circle were great places to reflect on work, social relationships and the environment. Always the interaction was dynamic and instructive.

"The greatest frustrations in the work were the delays in waiting for parts for the broken-down machinery. Also observing the excessive regimentation in the military social order was difficult to witness. A recognition that there existed a certain control and domination of non-patriot authorities also was frustrating for those of us who sought to identify with the local people. For some Pax men the yearning for mother's apple pie and other conveniences were frustrations.

"There was much to be learned mutually. To discover one another as members of God's large family was most rewarding. The cross-cultural learning in separate histories, separate family styles, separate economic views of life, national loyalties and notions of progress as represented by the construction of this highway were all part of the enrichment of our mutual relationships. Participating in the job itself and in off-work hunting forays helped to forge some strong relational ties.

"We often spent week-ends, holidays and fiestas, either by returning to the MCC Home in Asunción or hunting with local Paraguayan boys. There was a great deal of bantering, joking, morale boosting, writing to girl friends and reading the letters when they responded. We also learned to play games with our Paraguayan colleagues, did photography and occasionally visited the colonies.

"Since the Pax men came from a wide range of Mennonite backgrounds and regions it was an interesting and wholesome challenge to work together, to get to know one another, and to learn to respect variations in church life, in commitment to Christian service, and particularly such ideas as the peace witness and cross-cultural stances. Male quartet singing was one of the favorite pastimes of those who participated. There were also discussions on matters of faith, sometimes based on Bible study ventures. The unit life became somewhat of a faith-forging context that afforded insights gained from the surrounding culture, from the people themselves and from the contrast between North American and South American ways of life.

"Of particular importance was the visit on several occasions by colony administrators: Jacob Reimer of Menno, Heinrich Dürksen of Fernheim and Peter Derksen of Neuland. Along with President Stroessner they visited the project site, demonstrating the significant collaboration between the government of Paraguay, the Mennonite colonies of the Chaco, MCC, and the ranchers whose land was traversed. This seemed like an excellent four-way dynamic in getting the highway constructed. Working at close range with the Mennonite colony boys became an excellent opportunity for the Pax men to interact with and learn from one another.

"A Hunting Story"

"LaVerne Graber of Freeman, South Dakota, and I were joined by a Paraguayan friend, Roja, in a weekend hunt. We travelled by jeep a considerable distance into the jungle areas in order to hunt. We returned with a number of wild hens, a few chahá (a very large water fowl) and a wild gato (cat) about the size of a fox.

"What to do with the gato? Roja had the answer. 'I'll take it,' he said. And with that we parted company.

"That hunting day was so enjoyable that we decided to hunt again the next day, a Paraguayan civic holiday. Having ranged far from the base camp LaVerne and I remembered that we had forgotten to pack a lunch.

"At that point Roja opened up his maleta and offered us his galletas and cold meat. The food was delicious. The white cold meat, chicken we thought, was larger than most chicken breasts. When we asked Roja about the type of meat he replied, 'Well, that's the gato you guys gave me yesterday.' After a hearty laugh and a few rounds of tereré we felt just fine.

"A Night to Remember"

"It was August 15th, the day of celebration commemorating the founding of Asunción back in the 16th century. To celebrate properly, and especially to commemorate the big project – the construction of the Trans-Chaco highway – the government had requested that all road building equipment be brought into the city for a parade down Street 25 de Mayo. The earthmoving equipment was washed to perfection and wooden cleats placed on the bulldozer tracks. Then the Paraguayan soldier boys mounted the equipment and drove it down the streets. It looked magnificent.

"This was an occasion for me and my fellow Pax men to photograph this spectacular exhibit. But I made the mistake of joining the crowds wearing a bright red shirt and a white John Wayne-looking Stetson hat.

"The parade was still proceeding in full force when I felt a tug on my arm and a hand was placed on my camera. I was escorted, not exactly ceremoniously, from the stands right to the main street, and then marched between two military policemen against the flow of the parade. Together with a Paraguayan dressed in a dark green-blue suit I was on the way to captivity. We headed up the hill, around the corner and straight to a jailhouse. Once inside the police station the camera was confiscated and I wondered what the next move would be.

"In the meantime, friends in the stands who knew me, including fellow Pax guys, were wondering what had happened. I spotted my Pax comrade, Herman Konrad, who apparently was out looking for me, walking back and forth beside the open window facing the street. When the guards were not watching I looked out of the window and waved to him. Fortunately he saw me. When the guards were walking the other way I motioned him to come closer and spoke in Low German, telling him what happened.

"I was also minus my passport which I had not taken along, something foreigners visiting Paraguay were warned not to do. Herman departed without the guards noticing and returned a few hours later with my passport, brought from the MCC safe. Again, when the guard was walking the other way, he sneaked in through the bushes and handed me the passport through the window.

"Later that day my friend and I were escorted to a prison holding place. Guarded heavily by gun-carrying officials we were taken to the place of sentencing. Before the officials I was asked to account for my presence in Paraguay, my participation in the parade, and the heritage of my parents. When I said that my parents were born in Russia it was bad news. The fact that I was wearing a bright red shirt did not help my situation.

"Promptly I was sent back into the main part of the penitentiary which houses many others who had been arrested. I observed special prisoners being dropped into a deep cistern where escape was completely impossible. The ruthless treatment of the prisoners shocked me.

"Fortunately, Herman Konrad and others had discovered my whereabouts. Later that evening Herman and some Pax colleagues drove up to this jail by jeep and delivered some supper in the form of galletas and sandwiches and a bit of fruit. Herman had also brought me my poncho and another blanket to rest on. When night came I spread the poncho and blanket on the cement floor amidst unpleasant surroundings and actually fell asleep, only to awaken without the blanket under me.

"In the morning it was my job to sweep the latrine. The latrine was a scene of horrible stench and no place to walk, apart from trudging in the midst of human excrement and urine. "Clean this place up," was the instruction from the gun-carrying guard. "I have no broom," I replied. "Then make one!" he said.

"Having learned how to make brooms from my grandfather in the days when we lived in Reinland, Manitoba, I went to pick up some twigs, rolled them together, bound them as well as I could, and made a makeshift broom to do some cleanup.

"In the middle of doing a very unsatisfactory job I was whisked away by yet another set of guards who took me to the office and pinned a card on me which read, 'Detenido por 10 años' – Detained for 10 years. The sign gave me somewhat of a shock but there was no time to ponder.

"I was quickly placed in a vehicle, together with my fellow inmate, and taken to a downtown prison. Here I was questioned under fairly rough treatment by the guards. They insisted that our cameras would be opened and the films developed in order to discover what kind of spy activity we were undertaking. When I reported that my Kodachrome film could only be developed in North America they resisted opening the camera.

"We were then placed in confinement without food or other comforts. There we observed the kitchen staff through the holes in the wall and enjoyed the aroma of good food. And we actually wooed our way into obtaining some food from the kitchen staff, though it had to be done when the guards were not looking.

"By the time mid-day rolled around I was wondering if this was serious and whether the ten years of detention would have implications for MCC, for the Mennonite colonies, and of course, my family. With this realization I took the initiative, went to the guard, and told him I wanted to phone my consulate. His response was a strong jarring of his rifle against my rib cage. I also noted that the gun was cocked and that he was very firm in his demeanor. I insisted on one phone call, which was not granted. However, the jailer did agree to phone MCC and report my whereabouts to Director Frank Wiens.

"On receiving the call Wiens phoned the American and British consulates about my arrest. He also had an entree with the American representative, Mr. Babcock, who in turn had access to President Stroessner. It was this network of communication that ultimately resulted in some prompt action at the prison.

"By the time afternoon had rolled around the prison officials came to both me and my fellow inmate, asking us to appear at the front office and respond to further questioning. When we declared our identities both of us received profuse apologies from the officials and were released. Both of our cameras were returned to us with the explanation that we had been wrongly arrested.

"It was enjoyable to walk back to the MCC Home and to be greeted by Frank Wiens and the fellow Pax men. We celebrated with the drinking of tereré and with some freshly made popcorn. They even let me win a scrabble game that afternoon."

Clair Breneman (United States 1955–1957)

(Clair sent this report in 1997 from Indonesia, where he was working for MCC.)

"At first I was on the experimental farm in the Chaco with Bob Unruh. When the machines came I was transferred to the road. I worked from both ends of the project, building the road from Asunción and clearing jungle from the Chaco. I had a lot of farm equipment experience, but not heavy equipment experience.

"From the Asunción end we stripped off the top soil and excavated "borrow pits" where we would get clay and use it to build up the road. If we encountered a swamp area we would unload the dirt and push it into the swamp so it could then be driven on.

"There were usually 8–12 Pax men, several young men from the colonies and some personnel from the Paraguayan army. On weekends we would go to the Mennonite Home in Asunción where we interacted with the German Mennonite youth. We played a lot of volleyball. My main frustration was my limited ability in German and Spanish.

"From the northern (Chaco) end we cleared the jungle with D8 bulldozers in preparation for the road. I worked with Peter Harder and two young men from the colonies. A gentleman from Fernheim was our cook. We slept in a room that was mounted on wheels. We would move it with us as we progressed. On weekends we would come back to Filadelfia.

"The motivation for my work in Paraguay was to serve the church and our Lord. There was a draft at the time and I did not want to train for military service.

"We were a close knit group and had many memorable experiences – always prayers before meals and occasional times of sharing, praying and Bible discussions. On weekends we worshipped with the German Mennonites either in Asunción or in Filadelfia. I spent some vacation time with Menno Wiebe in Uruguay, Argentina and Brazil. We visited some of the Mennonite mission work, which was an influence on my life. In Curitiba, Brazil, we stayed with one of Menno's uncles whom he had never met before.

"A traumatic experience for me was the loss of two fingers. While unloading a barrel of diesel fuel I fell off the truck to the ground. The barrel landed on my hand and crushed four fingers. Pete Harder took me by jeep to the hospital in Filadelfia where I was treated. The following day a small plane came and transferred me to the Baptist Hospital in Asunción. A week later my two middle fingers had to be amputated because there was no blood circulation. The remaining two fingers are not flexible.

"The Pax men often played jokes on each other. On one occasion four of us went to a restaurant for ice cream. When we were finished the other three quickly left and I was the one who had to pay the bill.

"My name (Clair) was very hard for the Paraguayans to pronounce so I changed it to 'Antonio' and that was what I was called by the Paraguayans."

Robert Ediger (United States 1956–1958)

"We were the first group to work on the Trans-Chaco highway so there was lots of preparation work to be done. Equipment arrived slowly and some needed to be assembled. Our cook at the Asunción site was a Paraguayan and at the Chaco end it was a Mennonite. In my two years we cleared approximately 100 kilometers of right-of-way at the northern end and built 30–40 kilometers of road at the southern end.

"Growing up on the farm with lots of machinery and a Caterpillar for land levelling to enhance irrigation was of help to me. I also had a few weeks of training at the Peoria, Illinois, Caterpillar plant.

"I served in Paraguay to fulfil my alternative military obligations. I was also very interested in learning about a foreign country and a different culture.

"The road work was actually enjoyable. Living and relating to other Pax men was very rewarding. I found the Paraguayans to be very friendly and generous. We made some good friends.

"Most weekends were spent at the MCC Home in Asunción. We had some wonderful volleyball games, sometimes with the Mennonite youth groups versus the Pax group. Many rounds of 'Rook' were played.

"In the rainy season when we couldn't work on the road we would get all the equipment repaired and maintained, after which we were permitted to go hunting. There was a lot of wild game available. I shot two deer, lots of wild turkeys and some ducks.

"We attended the local church service, sang in the choir, and took part in other activities such as socials and youth group outings. All in all it was a good experience for me in Paraguay. Every time I visit Paraguay I still enjoy visiting friends like Adolf and Rudy Loewen and Helmut Siemens."

John H. Huebert (United States 1956–January 1958)

"With the building of the Trans-Chaco highway I began my service. I operated an earth-moving machine and also taught Paraguayans to operate it. I had no frustrations in my work. At home I had driven a D4 caterpillar leveling ground and trained for 2 weeks at the Caterpillar plant in Peoria, Illinois. For me this was alternative service in lieu of military training.

"On Monday mornings we had to get up early to catch the ferry across the Paraguay River to where the Trans-Chaco road started. We put in long days all week until Saturday afternoon.

"I enjoyed the company of other Pax men, working and playing together, worshipping together and sightseeing together. My girlfriend wrote me a letter once a week. My mother sent me a dollar in every letter she wrote.

"We mingled with the Paraguayans at work, and sometimes we visited people sitting in front of their homes. We had no trouble with the Paraguayans. If there was a conflict we would be taken to the police station right away and Frank Wiens would bail us out. I enjoyed the hamburger cookouts at the Frank Wiens home.

"For me the night we spent on the boat to Volendam was most memorable. We thought the night would never end. We had cabins reserved but it did not mean anything. There were people everywhere. It was cold and we did not have enough clothing. Two of us tried to keep warm under one blanket. We about froze to death. We ate pineapples until our mouths would get sore."

Virgil Claassen (United States 1959–1960)

"I arrived in Asunción in early May, 1958. Along with other MCC people, I first had to learn to operate the equipment and then train Paraguayans to run it. We had to make sure that the road was built correctly and were also responsible for keeping the machines in working condition. Training the Paraguayans was very difficult. I spoke no Spanish. Many of them were from the bush and did not speak Spanish either, only Guaraní, a local Indian dialect.

"During the two years I was there we worked on the road from Villa Hayes to Kilometer 101. This was a very difficult part of the road because there was a lot of rain and the ground did not soak up the water. We finally bulldozed the mud and water out to the sides and built the road in the middle.

"During the dry season we often worked two shifts so that work started at daybreak and went until dark. In the first year we crossed the Paraguay River by using a small ferry boat. At the end of 1959 a slightly larger boat was used.

"It was not always clear who was in control of building the road, MCC and the Paraguayan Mennonites, the Paraguayan government, the military or the Americans. Each group wanted to have a voice in the project. The US was investing the most money in the project so they thought they should be in charge. Most of the time, however, these persons stayed in Asunción and would come out one day about every two weeks to see the work, and give orders, which were not always realistic. We finally learned to agree with the US officials when they came out. However, when they left we went ahead and did the work the way we had learned from experience.

"One of the big problems was the rainy season. When it rained a lot we could not work. We were often kept busy doing repair work. Sometimes we had to wait 2–3 days or longer till the sun came out. I appreciated the Sunday evening faspa and service at the MCC Home in Asunción.

"When I came to Paraguay I was only 20 years old. Many of us were very immature but we got along well with each other and the Paraguayans. We enjoyed ourselves but we also worked very hard. When on the road project we lived simply. In summer it was very hot and in the winter it was cold.

"During vacation I was able to take trips to Argentina, Uruguay and Brazil where I saw the Iguazú Falls and visited the Mennonites colonies. It has been 37 years since I was in Paraguay."

Daniel Keith Yoder (United States August 1958–November 1960)

"I went to Paraguay so that I would not have to take military training in my homeland. I also sensed God's call to serve and help people in Paraguay. The rewards were very great. I feel I received more than I was able to give.

"My father owned an earthmoving and drainage business so I've operated a bulldozer and scraper since I was 12 years old.

"On the Trans-Chaco highway I did a lot of different jobs: driving the machines, repairing them, training others and doing whatever was necessary. In the evening a lot of time was spent swatting mosquitoes and trying to get them out from inside our mosquito nets.

"I enjoyed working with the Pax men, the Mennonites in the Chaco and the Paraguayans. Sometimes it was difficult to communicate because of the language barrier.

"The most frustrating times were when we were unable to work for extended periods because of too much rain; once it was three months. Another problem was that we sometimes had to wait for six months for a shipment of parts from the US.

"On most weekends we went to the MCC Home in Asunción. Later, as the work progressed, we were farther out and did not go as often. In Asunción we went to worship services, wrote letters, played games and slept later in the morning. We also did some volunteer work in Asunción during the extended rainy periods.

"The Bible studies we had as a unit were very rewarding. I also had personal devotions each day. My most rewarding vacation was a trip with another Pax man when we flew to Buenos Aires and then travelled by train across the Andes Mountains to the west coast of Chile."

Leslie Nafziger (United States September 1960–June 1963)

"I primarily did mechanic work on the machines. For a short time I was also cook for the Pax unit and occasionally operated some of the heavy equipment. At one point I drove a semi-truck, hauling everything from bridge timber to parts from Asunción. When the Trans-Chaco highway was finished I moved equipment and supplies from the Chaco to Colonel Oviedo to begin a new project. The last six months of my time I spent in Volendam on a MEDA dairy farm.

"I served in Paraguay since I did not wish to serve in the military in the US. I had no formal training for the work in Paraguay other than growing up on a farm in Ohio.

"I enjoyed living in another culture. The pace of life in Paraguay was much slower than what we were used to at home. But sometimes we were up before daylight and worked until dark. One of the frustrations was having to wait long for parts. We had to have a lot of patience in working with government officials.

"About once a month we would go to Asunción for a weekend where we attended the services at the German Mennonite church. From attending the young peoples' meetings and the German church services I learned to appreciate them and their history. During the rainy seasons we would try to get some of the machinery repaired. Sunday we usually wrote letters. Once a week we usually had a Bible Study and prayer meeting as a group. One reason I learned as much of the culture and history of the German-speaking Mennonites is the fact that I married one. At the end of my service I married Annemarie Federau, the daughter of Isaak and Erna Federau in Asunción. Because of that I have had the opportunity to return to Paraguay numerous times."

An illustration from a Sunday School lesson produced for the Mennonite churches in North America, on the theme: "Pilgrims in Paraguay." It seems that the illustration is intended to highlight the difficult situation of the Mennonites in the wild Chaco. The example of the "Pax-boys" who built the Trans-Chaco highway is intended to motivate others to volunteer for Christian service.

26

The Tran-Chaco Highway in the Context of a Practical Theology

In 1952 Harry Harder was asked how he intended to preach the gospel with a bulldozer. The person who asked this question likely saw no connection between a bulldozer and a practical living out of the gospel. Perhaps he wanted only to test Harder's motives, his reasons for going to Paraguay with a bulldozer to build roads for the Mennonites there. Unfortunately Harder has left no record of his answer to this question. It must have preoccupied the 36-year-old Harder a great deal, however. Many years later, shortly before his death on April 26, 1997, the 80-year-old still remembered the question vividly. He has taken his reply with him into eternity, but we can today reflect on what he might have thought at the time. Perhaps he did believe that a road that he was building could be a means of preaching the gospel.

Perhaps he thought too that even if he couldn't preach the gospel with a bulldozer, he could serve the Lord with one, inasmuch as it was a means of helping others. This thought comes through in some of his writings. Most likely his motivations were completely practical, to help others in need. In Paraguay there was need, and the doctor John Schmidt had told him that he would be able to help. He was persuaded by the need he saw in Paraguay, and so he went, motivated simply by the desire to help others. In doing so, he put into practice a theology, a profound religious conviction, that was deeply rooted in his community and the history of that community, the Biblical notion that faith and deeds must go hand in hand. *"So then, whenever we have an opportunity, let us work for the good of all, and especially for those of the family of faith"* (Galatians 6:10). *"Just as you did it to one of the lease of these who are members of my family, you did it to me"* (Matthew 25:40).

We may ask ourselves: What has the Trans-Chaco highway project to do with the Bible? Or, in other words: How is the practical theology taught by Mennonites expressed in the building of the Trans-Chaco highway?

First, through the Pax men. They saw their work on the Trans-Chaco highway project as service – as alternative service or as peace service ("Pax service"), which they did in place of military service. It is quite possible that not all of them were convinced that what they were doing was service or that it had theological implications. They were still young and inexperienced, after all. But the notion of service had been instilled in them by their parents and their faith community. In the construction of the Trans-Chaco highway, the notion of a theology of service came to practical expression. They earned no money for their work, rather, they served people and in so doing they helped these people to build a secure economic future. One of the consequences of their work was that the cultural and social life, as well as the charitable and missionary efforts of the colonies, were greatly strengthened. The extensive charitable and missionary work undertaken by the Mennonites in Paraguay would have been impossible without a healthy economic foundation, and this would not have come about without the Trans-Chaco highway.

Second, the Trans-Chaco highway project was conceived and brought to fruition by MCC; it was largely responsible for managing the project. The motto of MCC is "Service in the name of Christ." It is true that this motto was not prominently displayed during the building of highway, but it was the spirit in which the representatives of MCC served their fellow believers in Paraguay and thereby the Paraguayan people. This service in the name of Christ included offerings of time, finances, machinery and the volunteer work of many persons.

Finally, there is a 500-year history behind the Trans-Chaco highway project. It began with the Anabaptist movement in the 16th century and is grounded in the practical values and teachings of the Bible. In this sense, the history of this notion of service goes back to the Bible.

The Bible as the Basis for a Practical Theology

God desires that we put our faith into action, as the Bible makes clear. The Bible does not present a systematic theology, although this does have its basis in the Bible. We find throughout the Bible that God is constantly looking for ways to help humans and to make them happy. Theologians call this the redemptive purpose of God, which is like a red cord running through the entire Bible. Already in the Old Testament, God desired that his people would happily live together in peace and harmony. God knew full well, however, that humans are weak, and so God gave humans guidelines, practical commandments and instructions, that were intended to help humans to live together with each other in peace and harmony.

Of the many practical examples of these instructions, one is relevant for our purposes: humans in their relationship to material goods. Already in the Old Testament, God is revealed as the Lord of material goods. "The earth is the Lord's and all that is in it, the world, and those who live in it" (Psalm 24:1). God created the world and gave humans dominion over it, including the Chaco. But God remains the ultimate Lord of all material goods and all land on earth, not humans. "The land shall not be sold in perpetuity, for the land is mine; with me you are but aliens and tenants" (Leviticus 25:23). In Israel under the first covenant, the owners of land were not supposed to deal with their property as they wished, to buy as much as they could afford and to sell whenever and to whomever they wished. Rather, in order to maintain social balance, God gave the children of Israel concrete, practical instructions. On the one hand, private property was to be respected, but the arbitrary accumulation of land, possessions and wealth to the detriment of others was hindered by concrete rules. "Every seventh year you shall grant a remission of debts. And this is the manner of the remission: every creditor shall remit the claim that is held against a neighbor, not exacting it from a neighbor who is a member of the community" (Deuteronomy 15:1–2). Also, anyone who had been enslaved because of debt had to be set free. "For it is a jubilee; it shall be holy to you" (Leviticus 25:12). In a jubilee year, "you shall return, every one of you, to your property" (Leviticus 25:13). Property that had been acquired in the preceding seven years had to be returned to its original owners. By means of these practical regulations, social justice was to be maintained in Israel, that is, whenever the order was disrupted, it would periodically be re-established. God had the best of intentions for the people: social justice, the foundation for a comprehensive peaceful order, was to be the rule. Unfortunately, the people did not hold fast to these and other instructions. Here too the views of those who thought that Israel should be like other peoples came to dominate, to the great harm of the people of Israel. It was the judgment of the prophets that the misfortunes suffered by the people were the result of not obeying God's instructions. They lost everything.

According to the New Testament, God made another attempt to help humanity. The gospels recount that Jesus Christ came to bring the kingdom of God to earth (see Matthew 4:17; Luke 17:20; Romans 14:17). Within the new community, the community of believers, the kingdom of God was to find its fulfillment. This community would embrace every aspect of human life: the spiritual, social and economic. Jesus practiced this "Koinonia" with his disciples. The first apostolic congregations were also marked by this kind of community (Acts 3:43–47; 4:32–37; 5:1–11; 6:1–7). It was a community that encompassed everything, including material goods. "Now the whole group of those who believed were of one heart and soul, and no one claimed private ownership of any possessions, but everything they owned was held in common" (Acts 4:32). It was a voluntary community, in which no one was constrained by laws.

The notion of a community in which material goods are shared is also deeply rooted in Paul's theology. This principle comes to expression in the collection of money for the brothers and sisters who are part of the impoverished community in Jerusalem (see 1 Corinthians 16:1–4; 2 Corinthians 8 and 9; Romans 15:25–27). Paul encourages the churches he has founded to take an active part in meeting the needs of the mother church in Jerusalem.

Membership in the new community of faith also has a decisive impact on the relationship of Christians to their environment and fellow human beings, especially their fellow believers. More than this, a new way of living becomes noticeable. Christians should not live in luxury, or beyond their means, but rather follow a natural, moderate lifestyle. The primary purpose of work is no longer to become rich, but rather "so as to have something to share with the needy" (Ephesians 4:28). That does not mean, however, materially supporting those who are too lazy to work. Paul makes it very clear that "anyone unwilling to work should not eat" (2 Thessalonians 3:10). Responsible, believing Christians do not give thoughtlessly. They deliberate and plan where their material gifts can best be used. They have good ideas; instead of giving bread or money to the poor, they rather look for ways to help the poor earn their own bread. This is proper love of neighbor and practical development assistance motivated by faith. Contributing in this way brings joy. Generosity in doing good protects people from debilitating cares and leads to greater freedom (see Matthew 6:25–34; Luke 12:22 31; 1 Timothy 6:9–10; Hebrews 13:5–6). [50]

---

[50] For more on this theme, see Juan Driver, "Una Visión Bíblica de las Relaciones Económicos en el Pueblo de Dios," in El Evangelio: Mensaje de Paz (Semilla, 1984), pp. 34–45.

The Anabaptists and a Practical Theology of Service Rooted in the Bible

"The teaching of Christ is the decisive criterion for the Christian life" and "the life of Christ is a complete example for the Christian life." This is how J. A. Toews once formulated it. [51] This teaching was foundational for the Anabaptists of the 16th century, and applied to every part of life. They took the life of Christ and the apostles as the final rule for Christian faith and Christian life. Life and teaching were supposed to agree. They did not come up with a new teaching. They developed no new theology. They agreed with the major reformers of their time about all of the fundamental articles of faith. But they distinguished themselves from them in that they applied Christian teachings to the practical life of Christians. Once the truth of the Biblical teachings was recognized, it had to find reflection in deeds. "No one can truly know Christ, who does not follow him in life" (Hans Denck, 1500–1527). This led to the practice of baptism upon a personal confession of faith, following repentance and conversion. It also led Anabaptists to shun all acts of violence and to practice reconciliation and peace both in the community and with the world. "The gospel and those who follow it must not be protected by the sword, nor should the followers themselves do so. They do not take up the sword or practice war. Among them all killing is completely rejected" (Conrad Grebel 1498–1526). These ideas led them eventually to share their goods within the community and to use them to help others outside of the community as well. [52] They treated property as something given by God that was intended to be used for the good of the entire community. The principle of mutual aid has been passed down from generation to generation in Mennonite history, but regrettably has not been practiced often enough in that history with its many journeys. Abandoning this principle had negative consequences for the community – just as it had for the people of Israel. Mennonites often point out the similarities between the downfall of people of Israel and the end of the "Mennonite commonwealth" in Russia. In retrospect, many formerly wealthy Mennonites regretted that they did not make better use of their worldly goods in Russia to help others and to contribute to missions.

Menno Simons (1496–1561) wrote about this at length: "True evangelical faith is such that it cannot lie sleeping nor be at ease; rather it continually brings forth all kinds of righteous deeds that bear the fruit of love;

---

[51] J. A. Toews, *Wehrlos durch Christus* (Basel: Agape Verlag, 1964).
[52] For a thorough discussion of this theme, see Peter J. Klassen, "Mutual Aid among the Anabaptists: Doctrine." *Mennonite Quarterly Review* (April 1963), pp. 78–95.

it denies the needs of flesh and blood, roots out all forbidden desires and lusts, seeks and fears God and serves him from the depths of the heart; it clothes the naked, feeds the hungry, comforts the sorrowing, shelters the suffering, helps and comforts all whose hearts are weary, does good to those who have done it harm, serves those who have caused it hurt, prays for those who persecute it, teaches, encourages and chastens us with the word of the Lord, seeks out the lost, binds the wounded, heals the sick and protects the strong, it has become all things to all people." [53]

In 1553 Menno Simons found himself in Wismar with a few persecuted followers. At that time, Wismar was an important port on the Baltic Sea. In 1524, the city and its population had become Lutheran. An event that spelled the end of their stay in Wismar for Menno and the Anabaptists was the arrival of a ship full of Protestants (Calvinists) from England. Because of their evangelical beliefs they had been expelled by the English queen, Mary Tudor. They had initially set out for Denmark, hoping that the authorities, who were Lutheran, would give them refuge. To their bitter disappointment, however, they were forbidden to enter that country. So they set sail once again and on a cold December day they arrived on the coast of Wismar.

The rest of the story should be told in Menno's own words: "In the year 1553, shortly before the middle of winter, it happened that some of the brethren were told that a ship had come from Denmark, full of people who had been driven out of England because of their faith. They were trapped in the ice a short distance outside the harbor."

The Lutheran leadership of Wismar made no efforts to free the refugees from their unfortunate situation. The refugees followed teachings different from those of Luther, after all. When the Anabaptists heard about the situation, however, they hurried to offer the Protestants in need a helping hand. Menno continued: "When the brethren heard about the situation, they were overcome straightaway by a spirit of Christian mercy, which was only right and proper. They discussed this amongst themselves and diligently applied themselves (although they knew what the authorities might do as a result, which is in fact what happened) to help the Protestants caught in the ice and bring them safely into the city without awakening a disturbance. They brought wheat bread and wine with them, in case there

---

[53] *Die vollständigen Werke Menno Simons (Pfad-Weg Ausgabe, 1965), vol. 2, p. 349.*

were some among them who were sick or weak, so that they might strengthen and refresh them.

"After they had brought these people into the city, the brethren gathered 24 Thalers despite their own poverty and offered the money to the leaders of the Protestants (among them was Hermes Backerel, preacher), so that, if there were any who were in need, the leaders might use the money to serve the poor and help them in some way.

"They refused to take the money and said: 'We have money, we need only that someone help some of us to find work.' This our people did to the extent that they were able."

One of the Anabaptists even offered to take in the children of Johannes a Lasco, one of the Protestant theologians who belonged to this group but who had gone from Emden to London. To this Backerel responded that they couldn't take the children of an esteemed and highly educated man to have them live with and be cared for by common Anabaptists. A disappointed Menno remarked: "When I heard that, I realized that we had not welcomed among us simple, unsophisticated followers of Jesus Christ." [54] The principle, to help people in need, was passed along by the Mennonites from generation to generation and found concrete expression in many Mennonite relief organizations. The best known among them is Mennonite Central Committee.

The Mennonite Central Committee (MCC)

MCC was founded on July 27, 1920, in Elkhart, Indiana, in the United States, by a delegate assembly, to which most of the various Mennonite denominations had sent representatives. The occasion was the famine in Russia. The fellow believers there had to be helped. Food, clothing, and farm machinery were sent to Russia. At the height of their food distribution efforts, in June 1922, MCC was providing meals for more than 43,000 persons in kitchens built especially for this purpose. They sent bread to the houses of many others who were starving and also distributed many thousands of items of clothing to the poor. The cost of this effort reached US $1.16 million, but this was by no means the end of the help offered by MCC. Later, an additional US $25,000 were raised and spent to settle fellow

---

[54] *Die vollständigen Werke Menno Simons (Pfad-Weg Ausgabe, 1965)*, vol. 1, p. 551.

Mennonites in Paraguay and help establish them there. With the founding of MCC, the practical theology of the Mennonites, that is, the theology of service, as Peter J. Dyck called it, was established on a firmer footing and put into action. The work of MCC in Paraguay is good evidence of this. [55]

Peter J. Dyck has formulated the principle ideas on which MCC was founded. [56]

- The theology of MCC is biblical-Anabaptist in orientation.
- The service of MCC is done in the name of Christ and arises in response to human need and the call to Christian discipleship.
- The foundation of the work is not some philosophical theology but rather the earnest desire to be disciples of Jesus.
- Christ is our example. He did not come to be served but to serve.
- Our first task is to be co-workers with God in God's mission in the world.
- "Service is life." If we have an attitude of service in all our human relationships, we will live a genuine Christian life.
- Service for the Lord is an expression of thankfulness and love. "Let us love one another, for he first loved us" (1 John 4:19).
- Our deeds must match our Christian confession and testimony.
- Our deeds must be accompanied by verbal witness. Human relationships are of principle importance in our practical work.
- The practical outreach and missionary outreach cannot be seen as two separate activities. Dyck believes that previously Mennonites restricted their Christian witness too much to worship services and avoided verbal witnessing in their practical deeds. That was not right.

To return to the Trans-Chaco highway project. Because of the active and efficient intervention of MCC in the planning and construction of the Trans-Chaco highway, the Mennonites in the Chaco became the beneficiaries of the practical theology of MCC. But they should be more than beneficiaries; they should also model how to pass on these same principles of faith. Because of the Trans-Chaco highway, built by Harder and many Paxmen, it is now possible to distribute the Bible in many parts of the country

---

[55] *For detailed information on the service ministry and philosophy of MCC, see P. C. Hiebert and Orie O. Miller, Feeding the Hungry: Russia Famine, 1919–1925 (Scottdale, PA, Mennonite Central Committee, 1929), and John D. Unruh, In the Name of Christ: A History of the Mennonite Central Committee and its Services, 1920–1951 (Scottdale, PA, Herald Press, 1952).*

[56] *Peter J. Dyck, "A Theology of Service," Mennonite Quarterly Review 44 (July 1970), pp. 262–280.*

and to engage in practical Christian service. In this sense, the Mennonites in Paraguay feel themselves to be under a certain obligation. They have received a great deal of help. They now want to pass along this help to others and are doing so by means of many different projects: the work with the Indigenous peoples, neighborly assistance among Paraguayans, Christian service projects among those suffering from Hansen's disease ('leprosy'), those who need psychiatric care, with the physically handicapped and with street children. The work continues; it never stops. It began with one bulldozer. The gospel can be preached with one bulldozer!

27

Conclusion and Evalution

The purpose of this investigation was to use the available materials to describe the contribution of MCC and the Mennonites to the construction of the Trans-Chaco highway, and to account for what motivated them to do so. In conclusion the following points can be highlighted as especially worthy of being remembered:

1) The establishment of the Mennonite colonies in the Chaco, especially Fernheim and Neuland, was made possible because of the decisive actions of MCC. For this reason, MCC felt a large measure of responsibility for the Mennonite colonies in the Chaco.

2) These two colonies, as well as Menno Colony, founded in 1927, were locked for years in a life and death struggle for economic survival; for years, their future in the isolated Chaco seemed unlikely.

3) The colonies had been established in the midst of a wilderness that was almost completely cut off from the outside world. The isolation was felt particularly in the lack of a road connecting the colonies to a market. As long as this problem was not solved, there seemed to be no possibility of a secure economic future. The only solution was to build a road from the colonies to Asunción, the most obvious market for their products.

4) Because of its sense of responsibility for fellow believers in Paraguay, MCC kept up the search for ways and means to help the Mennonites out of a hopeless situation. Many attempts to do so failed. In the early 1950s, a road from the colonies to Asunción was an impossible

dream, a utopia. MCC and the Mennonites in the Chaco kept the dream alive until it became a reality.

5) Vern Buller, an American Mennonite, came as a volunteer to the Chaco and with the support of MCC and the Mennonites of the US he built approximately 135 kilometers of road from 1954 to 1955. The roads connected the colonies to each other and to the railway station Km 145. By building these roads, he demonstrated that fair-weather roads could be built in the Chaco relatively quickly and at low cost. Vern Buller's example was the catalyst that led to serious planning for the Trans-Chaco highway.

6) MCC took the initiative for the construction of the Trans-Chaco highway. The sources make this clear beyond a doubt. It was clear to MCC from the very beginning, however, that the goals of the project and the construction of the Trans-Chaco highway could not be restricted to the need to connect the Mennonite colonies to Asunción. The project was developed within a larger context, therefore, in order to gain the support of the American and Paraguayan governments: the goal would be the development of the entire Chaco, an increase in agricultural production and the expansion of cattle ranching and trade with Bolivia. This was the only way that the Trans-Chaco highway project would find national and international support.

7) The American development program Point IV became MCC's most important partner in the development of the project as well as in its implementation. Without the cooperation between Point IV and MCC, the Trans-Chaco highway would not have come into being at this time. The construction of this highway became one of the most important projects undertaken by the US in Paraguay. Documents from the US embassy make it clear that there too were individuals who felt personally responsible to bring together the Paraguayan government, the Mennonites and the Chaco cattle ranchers into an umbrella organization that would be responsible for carrying out this project.

8) The Paraguayan government (Chavez, Perreira, Stroessner) always supported the idea of the project whole-heartedly. Because road

construction in east Paraguay had priority, however, the building of the Trans-Chaco highway had to be delayed. When Alfredo Stroessner came to power, he acknowledged the initiatives already undertaken privately and, in November 1954, promised to build the Trans-Chaco highway. The Mennonites did not forget this promise.

9) The interest and the support of the Chaco cattle ranchers should also be highlighted. They committed themselves to contribute five million guaraní, a considerable sum at that time, for purchasing the fuel and oil needed by the road-building machinery. That this commitment was actually kept is thanks to the tireless efforts of Robert Eaton. Unfortunately, in the end they were not able to contribute the entire sum they had committed to providing. How much they did contribute can no longer be determined. The cattle ranchers, together with an American engineer, laid out the geographic route that the highway would follow. The land required for the highway was contributed at no cost by the owners.

10) The Training Project should no doubt be viewed as bait – as means to an end – since no supplies for the construction of the highway would have been made available from the US except for a project to train personnel in road construction.

11) MCC was the driving force setting in motion this large national project to build a Trans-Chaco highway. MCC took on the primary responsibility for the construction of the highway, at least for the stretch to the colonies – with the exception of one stretch on the north end that was built by Williams Brothers and the stretch of highway to Mariscal Estigarribia. It did so under the supervision of an American engineer.

12) The carrying out of the project proved to be much more difficult than anyone had realized at first. The low ground in the southern Chaco and the many rains had not been taken into account.

13) The Trans-Chaco highway made a decisive contribution to the economic development and a more secure future for the colonies. The growth of the dairy industry in the Chaco would be unthinkable

without the highway. More than 50% of the Paraguayan dairy industry is located in the Chaco.

14) From the perspective of MCC, the construction of the Trans-Chaco highway has to be seen in the context of the practical interpretation of the Bible and the application of its truths. The planning for and the construction of the highway were for MCC an expression of love of neighbor, shown especially in helping brethren in need.

15) MCC and the Mennonites in Paraguay were intimately connected by the same traditions and principles of faith and belief. The generous aid that the Mennonites in Paraguay received from their fellow believers obligates them in turn to help generously those who are in need. They are very conscientious about helping their neighbors within their churches and colonies but also beyond, practicing charity towards the Indigenous peoples and the people of the country.

28

A Personal Note in Conclusion

"How did it occur to you to write this book?" Many people asked me this question before the book was finally published. It occurred to me that I myself was no longer entirely sure why. There may have been a small degree of inspiration behind my decision. Alfred Hecht, professor of Geography at the University of Waterloo in Canada, reminded me in April 1997, when my research and writing was already underway, that I had told him years before that I intended to write about the "theology of the Trans-Chaco highway" sometime in the future. I had forgotten that I had said that. The thought has obviously been with me for a long time, however, although I am unable to say when it first occurred to me.

Perhaps the thought can be traced back to November 12, 1954, the date of the presidential visit to the Chaco. I was there, as a 13-year-old, with my father. I saw and heard the President of Paraguay right in front of me. His promise to build the Trans-Chaco highway is vivid in my memory. I can clearly recall the loud applause and the jubilation among the crowd of people present. An event like this was strange to me; it was something I had not yet experienced. I would probably not have remembered the promise made by the President if this promise had not been the topic of endless discussion and commentary among all of the Mennonites. Now when I look back, it strikes me how strong the hopes were for a Trans-Chaco highway. Even our teachers at school talked with the students about this and shared the dream with them. At the time, I had no clear idea about the significance that such a highway would have, but the lively discussion about a future Trans-Chaco highway, which would apparently be the decisive means of escaping a hopeless situation, has remained vividly in my memory, even though I have not done anything with these memories for decades. My memories were occasionally stirred as a result of contact with MCC representatives. I still have the tape recording of an interview with W. T. Snyder dating from 1973, in which he describes the contribution of MCC to the planning and construction of the Trans-Chaco highway. It was this interview that convinced me that MCC had played the decisive role in the construction of the Trans-Chaco highway, but I lacked the necessary supporting data. In our Mennonite circles I encountered widespread ignorance about the role played by Mennonites in the construction of the highway. On one occasion, I was even told by a well-known public figure that I would find no support for my thesis regarding the role of MCC and the Mennonites; the data demonstrating this existed only in my imagination. The highway had been a project of the government exclusively. It was upsetting to hear this.

Dr. Ramírez Russo, in his book on the Paraguayan Chaco, gives the Mennonites a great deal of credit for the contributions to the development of the Chaco, but even he mentions the "contribution of USOM and the Mennonites" only once when he describes the construction of the highway "from Villa Hayes to Filadelfia" and claims that the construction of the Trans-Chaco highway to the border with Bolivia was entirely the work of the Paraguayan government. [57] In the local history textbook published in 1975 for the Mennonites primary schools in the Chaco, the enormous significance of the Trans-Chaco highway is appropriately highlighted. But about the construction of the highway, the book notes only that "it was built through the cooperation between the Paraguayan government and the US." In the 1985 edition, the description of the significance of the highway has disappeared. There is only one bit of information: "The Trans-Chaco highway was important for opening up the Chaco." There is no mention of the fact that Mennonites were intimately involved in the construction of the highway. It is easy to conclude from this that the contribution of the Mennonites to the planning and construction of the highway was insignificant.

About fifteen years ago, in 1993, I decided to research and collect the sources and data for a history of the construction of the highway. I first contacted the offices of the CSEM (Comité Social y Económico Mennonita). Heinrich Dyck, the Executive Secretary, agreed immediately to have his secretary find the relevant documents and send them to me. This was in June of 1994. Unfortunately we found only a few documents. There was some correspondence from 1954 and the report of the auditors. For me, this report was, literally, shattering. My first impression found expression in the title of the chapters in which I describe the report: A Devastating

---

[57] M. Ramírez Russo, El Chaco Paraguayo: Integración sociocultural de los Mennonitas a la sociedad nacional (Asunción: Editorial El Foro, 1983), p. 153.

Judgment. I was even tempted to give up the project but eventually pulled myself together and wrote to MCC to ask them for the documentary data, especially the regular reports on the contribution of MCC to the construction of the Trans-Chaco highway. As I soon discovered, the reports had never been written. My initial efforts were proving to be fruitless.

A number of different thoughts went through my head. Could it be that MCC really had failed on this project? Why the silence? Was my project to write a theology of the Trans-Chaco highway simply a pipedream after all? I shared these concerns and questions with Frank and Marie Wiens during their visit to Paraguay. My concern must have made an impression on the Wienses. Not long after they had returned to the US, I received a letter from MCC with the news that they had photocopied several hundred pages of documents for me. In September 1994 I received the package which had been sent by airmail to Asunción. It happened that I was too busy at the time to read them all, so I filed them carefully, put them aside, and looked forward eagerly to my next holidays or a free weekend. I soon discovered that the material would be much more difficult to assimilate than I had expected at first. I found it very confusing, since I could find no point of entry into the material. Carefully I sorted it all: MCC correspondence, position papers, some newspaper reports, stories from the Mennoblatt, project proposals, contracts, etc. I began with the MCC correspondence and then worked backwards and forwards. I read each document, noted the most important points and copied them into my notebook. I read these notes again and again, I don't know how many times. The texts made reference to things that were obvious at the time, and for those who no longer know about these things, the texts will be incomprehensible. Who, for example, was LeTourneau. He is mentioned often, Pax-men worked for him, but there is no further information about him – those who needed to know at the time knew who he was. Edgar Stoesz and Frank Wiens were very helpful in answering these questions. The gaps in the materials also caused me no end of difficulty. I came to the conclusion that it would not be possible to write a comprehensive history of the Trans-Chaco highway project that would account fully for the contribution of MCC and the Mennonites. The information I had was like a jigsaw puzzle with many pieces missing. For the years 1959 to 1961, sources were completely missing. So I decided to put together the Trans-Chaco highway puzzle as best I could and fill in the details with the materials I had, while acknowledging the fact that much was missing. Then, at the beginning of 1997, when I thought my research and writing was almost finished, I received a quantity of new information, again through the kindness of Wiens and Stoesz. Linda Huebert Hecht of Waterloo, Ontario, in Canada, sent me a very informative series of articles that had appeared in the Canadian Mennonite. I was able to add a number of new chapters, and fill in some of the gaps. In a sense this book is a patchwork, pieced together from many different sources. For this reason it lacks a uniform style and a proper conclusion. This may disturb some readers, but others may find this appealing. I do think that a thread running through the whole is visible.

This book has taken a great deal of work, much more than I had anticipated or that readers might expect. On the other hand, this research has also given me a great deal of satisfaction. The time spent writing this book has given me many happy moments, and has inspired me in many ways. Often I was deeply moved. Once, for example, I was working on it close to midnight; it was very quiet, there was nothing to disturb me. For hours I immersed myself in the correspondence between Graber and Snyder. They were men of courage, they rarely complained. But they were struggling against a mountain of difficulties, and every so often their sorrow and longing comes through. There were many reasons for giving up, but they didn't do so. They knew that they were facing a decisive moment, and so they carried on. "In the name of Christ," they wanted to help their fellow believers, many thousand kilometers away in Paraguay. "In the name of Christ" they persevered. Many slept, unaware of their contribution, but this didn't discourage them. Nor did we in Paraguay fully understand what they were doing. We now enjoy the fruits of their work; they are dead and forgotten. But are they truly forgotten? No one set up a monument to their achievements, and I suspect they wouldn't want one. Their work remains to bear witness to them.

These thoughts and many others go through my head. I close my eyes and thank God that there are people like this. Their example enlightens and inspires me. I am grateful that we have examples like them in our faith community.

But to receive help also brings obligations with it. I often think back to my parents, who often said, when they came to Paraguay, that God had brought them there for a reason. Our brethren in MCC did not repeat these words to our parents merely to comfort them. With their prophetic vision, some of them saw that there could thrive in Paraguay a Mennonite "people" with a great mission: Bender, Unruh, Dyck, Wiens, Snyder, Stoesz and many others. As C. F. Klassen said in the beginning of 1948, when the Neuland and Volendam colonies had just been founded, "Remind those in Paraguay especially that they will play a role in the history of the Mennonites that we cannot even imagine yet. A great deal in the future of our history depends on how our communities in Paraguay are built up and what kind of witness they will be." [58]

We have a many-sided mission in Paraguay. We are in the process of carrying it out. The opportunities are everywhere around us. But our mission can be achieved for the benefit of all only if we allow ourselves to be led by the spirit of the Bible. All promises are conditional promises: they assume obedience, faith, perseverance and responsibility.

It is my hope that this book will help our Mennonite communities in Paraguay in three areas:

- to provide information about one part of our history;
- to cause reflection about our principles of faith; and
- to motivate our fellow believers and other citizens of this country to service.

---

[58] *"Zum Geleit." Der Mennonit: Ein Gemeindeblatt zunächst für mennonitische Neusiedler in aller Welt* (Basel, January/February 1948), p. 1.

Bibliography

(Archival sources – correspondence, reports, the texts of contracts and agreements, newspaper articles, and memoranda – are not listed here)

Bender, Urie. **Soldiers of Compassion.** Scottdale: Herald Press, 1969.

Bradford, William E. et al. **The Paraguayan Chaco.** Asunción, Paraguay: The United States Operations Mission to Paraguay, 1955.

"Changing Chaco, The." **The Mennonite** (August 25, 1964), pp. 510–513.

Dollinger, Gerhard. **Das Paradies in der grünen Hölle: Was ein Landarzt erzählt.** Stuttgart: J. F. Steinkopf Verlag, 1993.

Dyck, Peter J. "A Theology of Service." **The Mennonite Quarterly Review 44** (July 1970), pp. 262–280.

Fast, Heinhold. "Wie sind die oberdeutschen 'Mennoniten' geworden?" **Mennonitische Geschichtsblätter 43/44** (1985/87).

Fretz, Joseph Winfield. **Immigrant Group Settlements in Paraguay: A Study in the Sociology of Colonization.** North Newton, Kansas: Bethel College, 1962.

Pilgrims in Paraguay: The Story of Mennonite Colonization in South America. Scottdale, Pennsylvania: Herald Press, 1953.

"The Trans-Chaco Road." **Christian Living** (February 1960), pp. 1–7, 37.

Friesen, Martin W. **Kanadische Mennoniten bezwingen eine Wildnis.** Asunción, 1977.

Neue Heimat in der Chacowildnis. Altona, Manitoba, 1986.

Graber, Christian L. **The Coming of the Moros.** Scottdale, Pennsylvania: Herald Press, 1964.

Hack, Hendrick. **Die Kolonisation der Mennoniten im paraguayischen Chaco.** Amsterdam, 1961.

Harder, Henry M. "Northern District Brotherhood." **Mennonite Life** (October 1954), pp. 170–171.

Hecht, Alfred. **The Agricultural Impact of the Paraguayan Trans-Chaco Highway.** Working Paper no. 2. Wilfrid Laurier University, Waterloo, Ontario, 1974.

"Pioniere im Chaco Südamerikas: Indianer – Mennoniten – Paraguayer." **Marburger Geographische Gesellschaft e.V.**, Jahrbuch 1987. Marburg/Lahn, 1988, pp. 21–25.

"Regional Development. The Opening and Integration of the Chaco of Paraguay." **Research Paper No. 8243**, unpublished, 1981.

Hiebert, P. C., and Orie O. Miller. **Feeding the Hungry: Russia Famine, 1919–1925.** 1929.

Historia de la asistencia económica de los Estados Unidos al Paraguay, 1942–1992: Cincuenta años de cooperación para el desarrollo. Embassy of the United States of America, Asunción, Paraguay, 1992.

Im Dienste der Gemeinschaft. Published by the Council of Menno Colony for the 68th Anniversary of the founding of Menno Colony in the Paraguayan Chaco, June 25, 1995.

Janzen, A. E. **The Moro's Spear.** Hillsboro, Kansas, 1962.

Kempski, Dr. **Die Landwirtschaft im paraguayischen Chaco.** Buenos Aires, 1931.

Klassen, Peter James. "Mutual Aid among the Anabaptists: Doctrine and Practice." **Mennonite Quarterly Review 37** (April, 1963), pp. 78–95.

Klassen, Peter P. **Die Mennoniten in Paraguay: Reich Gottes und Reich dieser Welt.** Bolanden, Weierhof: Mennonitischer Geschichtsverein e.V., 1988.

Kleinpenning, J. M. G. **The Integration and Colonisation of the Paraguayan Chaco.** Nijmeegse Geografische Cahier No. 24. Nijmegen, Holland, 1984.

Man and Land in Paraguay. Latin American Studies 41. Amsterdam, 1987.

Rural Paraguay, 1870–1932. CEDLA Latin American Studies 66. Amsterdam, 1992.

Kohlhepp, Gerd. **Bevölkerungs- and wirtschaftsgeographische Entwicklungstendenzen in den mennonitischen Siedlungsgebieten des Chaco Boreal in Paraguay.** Tübinger geographische Studien, vol. 80. Tübingen, 1980.

Kühler, W. "Helfende Bruderliebe in der Vergangenheit seitens der holländischen Bruderschaft." In D. Christian Neff, ed., **Mennonitische Welt-Hilfs-Konferenz vom 31. August bis 3. September in Danzig.** Karlsruhe: Verlag Heinrich Schneider, 1930.

Neff, D. Christian, ed. **Mennonitische Welt-Hilfs-Konferenz vom 31. August bis 3. September in Danzig.** Karlsruhe: Verlag Heinrich Schneider, 1930.

Quiring, Walter. **Deutsche erschließen den Chaco.** Karlsruhe, 1936.

Im Schweiße deines Angesichts. Winnipeg, Manitoba, 1953.

Rußlanddeutsche suchen einen Heimat. Karlsruhe, 1938.

Ramirez Russo, Manfredo. **El Chaco Paraguayo: Integración sociocultural de los Mennonitas a la sociedad nacional.** Asunción: Editorial El Foro, 1983.

Ratzlaff, Gerhard. **Entre dos Fuegos: Los Mennonitas en el conflicto limítrofe entre Paraguay y Bolivia, 1932–1935.** Asunción, 1993.

Inmigración y colonización de los Mennonitas en al Paraguay bajo Ley 514. Asunción: Published by the Comité Social y Económico Mennonita (C.S.E.M.), 1993.

Regehr, Walter. **25 Jahre Kolonie Neuland, 1947–1972.** Karlsruhe, 1972.

Schmieder, O, and H. Wilhelmy. **Deutsche Ackerbausiedlungen im südamerikanischen Grasland, Pampa und Gran Chaco.** Leipzig, 1938.

Siemens, Nikolaus. **"Landespräsident Stroessner besucht die Mennonitenkolonien des Chaco (12. November 1954)."** Mennonitische Geschichtsblätter (1955), pp. 44–46.

Toews, J. A. **Wehrlos durch Christus.** Basel: Agape Verlag, 1964.

Unruh, John D. **In the Name of Christ: A History of Mennonite Central Committee and Its Services, 1920–1951.** Scottdale, Pennsylvania: Herald Press, 1952.

www.ingramcontent.com/pod-product-compliance
Lightning Source LLC
Chambersburg PA
CBHW072133160426
43197CB00012B/2089